IGNITE YOUR RESEARCH MOJO

IGNITE YOUR RESEARCH MOJO

How you can make user research impactful and transform your company

Dilip Chetan

Illustrated by Ben Crothers

ISBN-13: 9781979571746
ISBN-10: 1979571740
Library of Congress Control Number: 2017917554
CreateSpace Independent Publishing Platform
North Charleston, South Carolina

To the phoenix

Fly high and you burn
Yet you reach for the sun, fool
Unbelievable.

Table of Contents

Acknowledgments

I never intended to write a book on research. I didn't think I had enough material to write a book. I used to be under the impression that anything I wanted to say on the topic of user research could be put in a single page. I mean, what could I say about user research that hadn't already been said? Except for one thing—no one seemed to fully address why research projects were failing, and why the best of companies, that seemed to get everything else right (for the most part at least) failed so miserably when it came to making use of research data. So I thought I'd write a blog about it. I started looking around for instances where research completely failed, and realized that there was way more material than would ever fit in a single blog. That's when the idea of writing the book came to me. So it goes without saying—in many ways, I owe this book to the numerous research projects I have been a part of or witnessed in my career, to the researchers who conducted them, and to the stakeholders who consumed the research findings (or didn't!).

Writing a nonfiction book is hard, even if a lot of it is based on my own experience. My writing not only took a toll on my schedule, it also was something that impacted my family significantly. But, like the troopers that they are, my wife and kids stood by me every step of the way. My wife held the fort admirably and took over a lot of things that I do around the house so that I can have time to write. This book is just one small example of the innumerable things in my life that would not have been possible without her. I am also eternally grateful to my twin children. Even though they are just 15 years old at the time of writing this book, they have helped me in many ways with the book, including giving me suggestions on chapter titles. I owe quite a bit of the humor in this book to them.

Speaking of humor and people who are good at it, how awesome are the images in this book?! They all came from the incredible brain of one man—Ben Crothers. Ben has more talent in his left pinkie toe than most people have in their entire bodies. And he is not afraid to put that talent to good use, like he did in this book. Ben was able to bring to life some incredibly hard concepts with his clever sketches. Ben can make a research book as much fun to read as a graphic novel! Thank you, Ben, my brother from another mother.

In addition to my incredible family, I am also blessed with some amazing friends and coworkers, some of whom helped me get this book to where it is now. I would be remiss if I don't thank them. Sanjeev Kriplani, you read the initial draft of the manuscript during your vacation (who does that!!) and gave me feedback that altered the direction of the book. My designer buddy and Resident Greek God Konstantinos Giannakis, thank you so much for your suggestions! Glen Abrahams, your input has gone a long way in shaping the cover of the book; huge thanks to you! Then, there is my bff Mary Trombley, whom I have known for nearly a decade now. Mary, you gave some crucial feedback on this book. You and I have worked together in two companies so far, and I can't wait to work with you again!

Introduction

Mortimer Doormatt Snipple (I made up this name to protect his identity) is a close friend of mine and a fellow user researcher. He works for a Fortune 500 company in the Bay Area of California. Thirty-four-year-old Mort, at six feet three inches tall, is a lean, handsome man with impossibly high cheekbones. He has a PhD in human factors of systems and product design from Virginia Tech. Mort is a quiet, thoughtful man, and behind the frames of his steel-rimmed glasses, his sharp, piercing eyes are testament to a wisdom that belies his age.

Mort loves research. Every aspect of it. He wakes up every morning with one wish—that today will be the day he will uncover an insight that will blow everyone away. He goes to bed every night hoping that day will be tomorrow. Mort provides research support to one of the company's massive financial products, the roadmap of which is owned by Rob Doesntgivetwohoots.

Rob is a brilliant man with the fascinating job title of senior product manager. Highly competitive by nature, Rob is driven by one thing—getting a promotion within the next six months. With this promotion, he would become the lead product manager and get a shot at managing a small team of product managers. And he sees Mort as his ticket to climbing that ladder.

Rob has poured his blood, sweat, and tears into coming up with some great features for the financial product. He knows how the customers think and what they need. He hasn't spoken or interacted with any of them. But that doesn't matter. He knows how they think and what they need. He just does.

The problem is, his boss doesn't seem to recognize Rob's genius. Rob needs to prove that he is on the right track and that he has been all along. That's where Mort comes in. Rob figures that if he can get Mort to validate the basic assumptions underlying his feature set by running some user sessions with a bunch of customers, he can justify himself to his boss.

Mort, ever in search of the Great Insight, is eager to help Rob, even if he doesn't agree with Rob's motives or the fact that Rob only wants to use Mort to validate his assumptions. Mort comes up with a research plan. He recruits from the right user profiles, from the right geographic locations. He combines both quantitative and qualitative testing methodologies. He asks the right questions, formulates the right hypotheses. He prepares a test script that addresses all the concerns of Rob's team. He keeps the stakeholders informed throughout the process and solicits their input, which he diligently incorporates into his research plan.

He makes sure all the key stakeholders attend the sessions and debriefs them at the end of each session. Then he conducts a workshop where he presents actionable insights and makes sure appropriate engineering resources are identified to bring the insights to life in the product. Mort is overjoyed. A couple of insights are pretty damning. They show that two of the key features Rob had in mind were actually not what the customers would find useful. He is concerned about how Rob will receive this information. But to his surprise, Rob takes everything in stride. He even thanks Mort publicly at the end of his workshop for a job well done. Mort is overjoyed.

Six months pass. Rob is now a lead product manager and is overseeing a team of four product managers in two locations. Mort is still a user researcher. Funny, his insights never really seemed to make any impact on the product. Oddly enough, the very features that Mort campaigned against are now the key features being touted as part of the CEO's keynote in the company's big annual conference.

This book is born from pain.

I have worked as a user researcher in different companies, and rarely have I seen effective research being conducted anywhere. By "effective research" I mean research that significantly impacts product. (Just to be clear, I'm not talking about quality of research here, although that is a crucial part of being effective too, and I'll cover that later in the book.)

What's more, I have lots of researcher friends in some of the top companies in the world, and they all agree that in most cases, user research has little impact on the product. A lot of these companies spend top dollar in hiring the best researchers from the best schools across the country. Some of them even build elaborate usability labs (the ones with one-way mirrors and expensive video cameras, and monitors with software that lets you see users' faces while they are using the product). Still, there is one problem. The research conducted at such facilities has little or no impact on the products the company makes. It kind of "dies on the table."

What's going on here? Whatever it is, it's not for lack of trying. User research (or usability engineering or usability science or user experience research, whatever you want to call it) does get a fair bit of attention these days. Even people who have no idea what it really is have found that it is cooler to say "we conduct user research on our products." And researchers are busy, by and large. They keep doing something every day, and work hard at it.

The problem is, when you ask them what happened with all that research, they don't have a clear answer. How much of that research actually led to some meaningful insights? And how many of those insights actually led to some real changes in products or processes? Come to think of it, how many researchers do you know who can clearly articulate tangible impact from their work? When I talk about tangible impact, I don't mean ROI in dollar terms. I honestly believe that's a stupid way of assessing research impact, and I'll talk about it in greater detail in chapter 15. Nor do I mean changes like altering the terminology and color of a button on an obscure web page. What I mean is, can you clearly draw a connection between what the researcher uncovered and a significant change made to a product roadmap?

It's pretty challenging, and I applaud the user researchers who can actually demonstrate this. The reason it's so challenging is that when it comes to research, the information generally flows just one way. Researchers are very good at communicating the insights they uncover and even at coming up with good recommendations on how to incorporate their learnings in a product. But the second part of the flow is missing—getting the business to commit to incorporating the recommendations and then reporting back on how the research was used and whether or not the findings made sense. In most cases, this happens because user research is treated like a bureau, not an integral part of the cycle. Researchers are like the managers of a rock band on tour. They are a huge part of the why the concert is a success. But they don't make the headlines. They seldom get invited to the after-party. And they don't get groupies running after them.

According to the late Steve Jobs, former Apple CEO, and someone who is revered like a god in the Bay Area, you don't hire smart people and tell them what to do; you hire smart people so they can tell you what to do. Guess that is especially lost on people who work with researchers. There is no end to the list of people who have opinions on what should be done with research, or even with researchers themselves! When it comes to research, everyone becomes an expert, and everyone has ideas and opinions about it, and everyone loves to share these ideas with researchers! People, it appears, love to tell researchers what to do. But no one seems to listen to researchers when *they* try to say something. Then why even invest in research in the first place?

I asked this very question of a bunch of product managers and design managers. Here are some of the most common answers:

We listen to customers.
We do "user-centered design."
We need a better understanding of where the market is headed.
("We aim for not where the puck is, but where it's going to be"—
heard that before?)
We want to be proactive.
We anticipate customer needs and satisfy them even before our
customers realize it...

Cheesy as some of these answers may sound, at least they show that the managers' hearts are in the right place. Now what about the researchers' skills and education? Do they have the right skill set to meet the challenges at hand?

Researchers come from a variety of backgrounds. There are the more traditional researchers who have a master's degree or a PhD in a branch of psychology. Human factors, cognitive, or social psychology are the most common. Researchers could also have advanced degrees in human-computer interaction. Many also come from the behavioral sciences and even the consumer behavior side of marketing.

Then there are some nontraditional degrees. I have come across successful researchers with degrees in everything ranging from journalism and commerce to industrial engineering, law, and geography! But that's OK. Whether or not they have formal degrees in human factors or other branches of psychology, most researchers learn on the job, and they eventually get pretty good at understanding and implementing different methods of research.

It seems that companies are genuinely interested in investing in user research. And there seems to be no dearth of good user researchers either (at least in some companies). So where are the rock-star user researchers who have transformed products in their companies, and why are so few of them in the limelight? In fact, where are the products that got transformed by virtue of some great user research? And why is it so hard to find a good connection between research and the products that it influenced?

PURPOSE OF THIS BOOK

That's where this book comes in. This book is divided into three parts.

The first part is for anyone who is looking to run research. This can be a formally trained researcher or a product manager, designer, or engineer seeking to run some research on the side. This section looks at some of the common mistakes they make when they set out to do research (like failing to ask the right questions or not knowing how to formulate a hypothesis, etc.). We then examine the ways in which research can be conducted so it has maximum impact. We cover everything from asking the preliminary questions to getting insights and turning those insights into something actionable.

One thing we will not be covering in this section (or in the entire book, as a matter of fact) is user research methods. There are plenty of books for that. A simple Amazon or Google search will bring up a plethora of books on methods. This book is meant to augment those methods books. The purpose of this book is to show how any company can make use of user research and transform itself into an evidence-based, decision-making powerhouse, and how you as a researcher can lead that transformation.

The second part of this book is addressed at a slightly more experienced researcher. Here, we examine the importance of researching emotions, identify what bad research is and how to recognize and avoid it, and explore the main things researchers can do to have a meaningful impact in their organizations.

The third part deals with some of the broader reasons why user research is not as effective as it should be in many companies, even if those companies have high-quality researchers who do their jobs well. In this section, we'll talk about things that may be beyond the researcher's control but which can have a significant impact on whether or not research will succeed in the company. We look at a fundamental flaw in product-development philosophy—and how to avoid it. We also look at factors like company culture, hiring the right researchers, building a career map for them, organizing them in teams, and, finally, how to assess the value of their work in terms of ROI. The basic philosophy here is that if the company takes good care of research, research will take good care of the company. For your convenience, I have also indicated who each section of the book is addressed to along with the section headings.

See, the main premise of this book is that just knowing the techniques is not enough to conduct successful research and create value in your organization. There's a lot more to it. Any company that's been doing this for a while knows that. This book helps you jump headlong into the murky waters of what happens before and after research methods are implemented. It helps you understand the complex world of project management, organization culture, effective communication, crazy deliverables, and the *je ne sais quoi* that exists in modern design decision-making.

In short, this book will help you understand everything you need to navigate in order to make you realize the full power of research in your company. And with that, I'm going to step off my soapbox. On to chapter 1.

Part 1
Doing good research

This section is for people who like to do a little research on the side, for people getting started in a formal research role, and for people who are already experienced with research but are always open to the possibility of learning something new.

1

Allow myself to introduce...
myself...and my mojo!
Defining the mojo

"User research is just glorified QA."

—Product manager

"The product manager tells you what to test. The customers give feedback on our products. The designer creates the UI based on test findings. So what exactly do you do again?"

—VP of product management to a user researcher

WHAT IS USER RESEARCH?[1]

For the sake of simplicity, let's consider product companies (as opposed to service companies). I looked up the definition of user research from a lot of sources. I didn't like any of them. So I'm giving you my own definition. *User*

---

1 User research has also been called various things like user experience research, human factors research, experience research, design research, etc. I am going with user research in this book because that is the zeitgeist of today.

research is the science that helps us understand the causes and manifestations of user behavior and the resulting interactions of users with their environment.

From a practical (i.e., corporate) standpoint, user research operates at three levels.

1. The user. I use this term a bit loosely. I mean it to include not just the end user, but all the other people who interact with your company and your products in one way or another. It could be one individual or a team of people.
2. The product. For convenience, let's just consider a physical product instead of a service of some sort. Note that service is also covered in the definition, but we are just not using it for now.
3. The interaction between the user and the product in a given context.

User research is the science that helps us understand the causes and manifestations of user behavior, and the resulting interactions of users with their environment.

Let's go a little deeper into these three levels.

The user

Understanding people and their underlying motivations, aspirations, and behaviors is critical. Without this, you won't get a handle on the most impor-tant part of the equation—the customer. The thing about people is that they don't always articulate their wants and needs. Many times, they might not even be aware of their wants and needs. User research provides a host of tools—like personas, behavioral observations, and task analysis—all tailored to get deeper into users' psyches and reveal what they would really appreciate. User research also helps us understand the different players in the game—all the way from the evaluator and purchaser to the end user.

The product

As I mentioned in the previous page, I'm going to be talking about a product here. But remember that everything I speak about in this book can be translated just as easily to any service, like health care, hotels, or professionally facilitated cuddle parties (that's a real thing!). User  research helps ensure that you never think about the product you're building without thinking of the user first. It provides insights that let you build a better product at every stage, from figuring out information architecture, to sketching on a napkin, to creating wireframes and prototypes. There are a whole bunch of techniques specifically tailored to answering the right question at the right stage of product development. User research helps bridge the gap between what you *think* the customer needs and what the customer *really* needs. It provides valuable data about behaviors, usage patterns, and customer journeys that all contribute to more intelligent decision-making regarding anything you choose to build.

The user-product interaction

This is the final piece of the puzzle. It's not enough to build a product in isolation. You need to build the product so it is perfect for the customers. This means understanding how the user interacts  with the product and figuring out how to design a product that feels natural and intuitive, leading to a delightful user experience.

WHY SHOULD I DO USER RESEARCH?

Because if you don't do it, you'll end up building stupid things like the motion-sensing faucet and its counterpart, the automatic flushing toilet.

STEVE JOBS DIDN'T DO USER RESEARCH. BUT HE BUILT AWESOME PRODUCTS. SO, AGAIN, WHY SHOULD I DO USER RESEARCH?

Sadly, I've actually been asked this question many times. I usually don't dignify this with an elaborate answer. First off, do you have a really deep, inherent understanding of your users and their needs? My sense is that Steve Jobs did. His objection to research may have been that that users can't always tell us what they want, which is true. But Steve probably had a very intuitive understanding of what his customers needed. Also, there is no proof that he didn't strive to understand users and their behaviors in some way or form while coming up with product ideas. Second—and pay close attention to this—you are not Steve Jobs.

————

Pay close attention to this—you are not Steve Jobs.

So you need to do research. If you don't, you'll end up building stupid things like the motion-sensing faucet and its counterpart, the automatic flushing toilet.

WHEN SHOULD I DO USER RESEARCH?

You should do research every time you need to make an informed, intelligent decision. I hope for your sake that this is all the time. It doesn't matter how big or small the impact of the decision is. Any time you need more information (data) to make a decision, you need to do research.

There is a decision to be made every time you face a need to come up with the next course of action—every time you ask "what do I do next?" Decisions can be as mundane as "do I wear the brown shirt or the black shirt?" (some quick research into fashion trends would help—maybe brown is the new black?) or as complex as "do I sell my company and cut my losses, or do I come up with a plan to save my business even if it means losing some more money in the short term?" The second question would of course need a whole lot more research, and a good bit of it would be focused internally. Different companies do user research under different conditions and during different phases of product development. I'll illustrate this with an example.

BART (Bay Area Rapid Transit) is a major commuter-train system in the Bay Area. In 2015, around 423,000 people rode on this train system every weekday. BART connects San Francisco with cities like Oakland, Pleasanton, and Fremont in the East Bay. According to its Wiki page, as of 2016, BART operates five routes on 104 miles of track, with forty-four stations in four counties. That's pretty extensive, although not nearly enough to ferry the Bay Area's burgeoning population to its offices.

Like many other train systems in this country, BART is pretty old. And some of the train cars date back to the '80s. For a few years now, BART's management has been considering expanding and modernizing its fleet. However, as in many large-scale government projects, budget is rarely available on time. Since a system as elaborate as BART cannot just keep scaling all the time, they need to make sure the schedules are optimum and the manner in which the seats are configured meets the ever-growing demand from Bay Area residents.

———

You should do research every time you need to make an informed, intelligent decision.

So, BART does some extensive user research, consisting of detailed surveys about ridership patterns and the experiences its riders have on its trains. This research comes in the form of its Station Profile Survey (1). BART has run this survey fourteen times since 1973. In place of the paper surveys that were administered previously, the latest one, in 2015, included interviewer-administered surveys on tablets—which meant there was increased interaction between interviewer and respondent.

BART also came up with new prototypes for its fleet of cars of the future. And this is where another part of the user research they conducted comes in. The good folks at BART placed the train cars at strategic stations along different routes. Riders were invited to check them out and give their feedback (2).

To summarize, the people at BART conducted some early-stage exploratory studies to understand its user needs. They then understood the context in which different users traveled, and what their pain points were. They used these inputs to design new cars. Once the prototypes were ready, they conducted further research on them.

There is really no stage in product development when research cannot be done (3). In fact, you can do research even to figure out what to build. For instance, let's say you have a general idea that you want to build a productivity-enhancement tool for the workplace. But there are plenty such tools available already. And you really don't know what aspect of productivity you want to enhance. You also don't know who your end users are likely to be.

I have actually seen this situation in some companies. Where and when is this most likely to occur? Consider a company that has gotten really, really famous by making just one product. Any companies come to mind? Now, this company coasts on the success of its one product for a few years. Sooner or later, tongues will start to wag. People wonder if this is all the company is capable of ever producing. Then the CEO has a word with his CTO. The CTO speaks with some product heads, and soon a whole bunch of people are tasked with building the next awesome product for the company, but nobody knows exactly what to build—or even how to go about the product-envisioning process.

In such cases, companies come up with "new" products that are minor variations of their one hit—or, worse, totally different products that create a chasm in the company. Pretty soon, they put the whole company in a tailspin. Smart companies recognize this early on and ditch the new product before it does too much harm. Other companies continue on, throwing good money after the bad, until eventually they crack under pressure and put themselves up for sale.

But some companies actually make this transition effectively. How do they do it? Or the more relevant question is—how can you do it? How can you figure out what the next great product should be? And how can user research help?

Going back to our example, let's say one of the product heads has enlisted the help of his team's researcher in trying to figure out what to build next. The researcher starts looking to see what kind of productivity-enhancement tool people would appreciate. Since the tool is going to be designed for the workplace, it's pretty obvious that she needs to conduct her research at different kinds of workplaces. She starts by selecting an industry where the tool would be applicable. Let's assume her company currently makes a product for the health-care industry. So she decides to focus her research on a similar demographic. Her team has decided there is no sense is going very far from the company's core competency. The company currently makes a scheduling tool for doctors and nurses. It only makes sense for the productivity tool to apply to the same industry.

The researcher has two months to come back with her findings. She starts by mapping out a list of clinics she is going to be visiting. Many of the clinics are local (within a twenty-mile radius), and others are in selected locations across the state. She visits each of these clinics for a few hours over a couple of days. She becomes a fly on the wall and starts recording her observations.

That is the best kind of research, really. It's great because it happens under real conditions, not in the laboratory. The methodology is simple: the researcher simply observes. Of course, she needs to have some basic idea about what to observe, and whom to observe, and even *how* to observe.[2]

---

2 The *how to observe* thing is surprisingly difficult. I've been going on site visits with many people from different divisions over the years. One thing I've observed about the observers—stay with me here—is that people don't know how to observe quietly. They keep interrupting,

She also complements her studies with quantitative techniques and some big-data she was able to procure via third-party vendors. She subjects all the data she has collected to intense analysis. She starts noticing something interesting. She discovers that most clinics seem almost unprepared for certain kinds of disease outbreaks. They are usually prepared for some of the more common, seasonal diseases like the flu. But when it comes to certain less common outbreaks (like strep throat, for instance), she sees a pattern in which clinics get overwhelmed pretty quickly. This in turn cascades into longer wait-times, overworked hospital staff, and angry patients.

She comes back to her company and makes her recommendation: they should build an app that studies seasonal symptoms in people. Incorporating data provided by organizations like the CDC, the app could make educated predictions about the likelihood of a certain kind of outbreak occurring in the near future.

The company could build two versions of this app—one for the hospitals and clinics themselves, and the other for patients. In both versions, the users would be forewarned about the possibility of an outbreak occurring. Hospitals could use this app to help them predict and schedule more efficiently. They would be better prepared for the outbreak and make sure that adequate staffing resources were on hand to handle increased patient load. The average person would also be better prepared to take better care of his or her health and avoid behaviors that could lead to increased vulnerability to the outbreak (for instance, helping people make more informed decisions on what to eat or drink).

The researcher has brought back data. She has analyzed the data and made her recommendations. She has also validated that both clinics and patients love the idea. It is now up to her company to decide how they could build the app.

Once the product team is on board, it's only a matter of time before more research is required. For instance, there needs to be a much clearer

---

asking questions. If only people would realize they can learn a lot more by just shutting the hell up!

understanding of the personas[3] who would be using the app. They need to figure out what features make it into the app and at what price point the app should enter the market. Then there is the more standard concept testing and usability testing of prototypes. I guess I have made my point. Research can pretty much be done at every stage of product development, and before product development even begins!

Now, let's look at the other side of the coin.

SOMETIMES, IT'S OK TO ACTUALLY *NOT* DO RESEARCH.

You read that right, folks. I came out and said it. And I believe it so strongly I'm going to say it again: sometimes it's OK to actually *not* do research. Some of you researchers out there may let out a horrified gasp. That's OK. This is as good a time as any to get that gasp out of your system.

When a company hires product managers and designers, part of their job is to envision the product in its entirety. From start to finish. And even if you are a researcher, you must admit—maybe grudgingly, even—that oftentimes, the product managers and designers deliver exactly what the doctor ordered. How is this possible? Isn't user input critical for building great products? Don't you have to identify the user wants and needs and derive product features and design decisions from them? Yes, yes, all that is true. I don't deny that, even for a minute. But here's what I'm saying—research isn't *always* required. There are such things called "creative genius," "experience," and that all-encompassing term "gut feel." When the stars align, these things do something amazing. They reach for and touch the sky.

Creative genius

At heart, a designer is an intuitive and creative person (4). She should be. Her job demands that. A designer has the innate ability to look at a problem and come up with a design that effectively solves the problem. And that's the key right there—"effectively." The solution should be aesthetically pleasing,

---

3 A persona is an archetypal user who has a set of characteristics that represents a particular population. For example, you could come up with a persona that would represent founders of tech startups. This persona could embody the common behaviors, investment choices, and decision-making styles common to founders of tech startups.

easy to understand and interpret, simple to learn and use, withstand the rigor of usability testing and, above all, be practically viable; people should be able to build and implement it. This implies the following.

––––––––

Research isn't *always* required. There are such things called "creative genius," "experience," and "gut feel." When the stars align, these things do something amazing, and they can take the place of research.

The designer understands the problem space accurately. She knows the exact conditions under which the problem occurs and the consequences of not solving the problem. Next, she understands exactly who is affected by the problem. This includes understanding all the personas involved and knowing their pain points, and what they really need or want. More importantly she should have a sense for honing in on that unmet, unarticulated need and then know exactly how to solve for it. For instance, no one explicitly asked for GPS-based navigation on their phones. But since this feature was introduced in smartphones, it has become virtually indispensable.

Does that sound like a whole lot of baloney to you? I can tell you for a fact—such designers do exist. And they deliver impeccable, elegant solutions that blow one's mind. And what's more, a lot of companies employ such designers. They are all around you. Just look around. In some cases, it's usually just one rock-star designer. In other cases, like that of the iPod design team, it's a whole group of designers. But creative design exists. Creative designers exist. And a lot of them didn't come up with their designs by actually starting with user research. Their creativity took care of it all.

It goes without saying, of course, that not all designers are this creative. But they do come up with clever innovations during their jobs, and not everything they build needs to be subject to user testing. Sometimes you should just go with your gut and let designers' creativity shine through, without being influenced by research data all the time. This is especially true with things like the impact of aesthetics, which are incredibly hard to fathom. Some really cool design features may not even stand up to the rigors of usability testing. Doing away with such features may be detrimental to the success of the product itself.

Also, testing things like color schemes and whether a given box should have rounded or sharp edges is, in most cases, a huge waste of time. Such things should not be tested. My advice to researchers: leave aesthetics to the designers. You don't have to butt your head into every little thing created by a designer. There are a lot of other fish for you to fry.

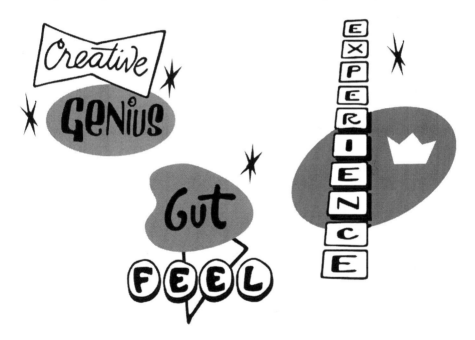

Experience

This is the part of my book where I raise my hat to people with experience, because I've seen them do some pretty awesome things—purely by virtue of the fact that they've done stuff in the past and have learned from their mistakes. And everyone else in the company should pay attention when experience speaks. Even designers and researchers.

I still remember. It was during my rookie years as a researcher. I ran some studies and came back to the product team with my findings. I was in a room with a bunch of people connected to the product—product managers, designers, even a couple of sales folk. Some of them were pretty experienced and had been with the product many years. A couple of them were from the team that conceived the product many years ago.

They all sat quietly, even respectfully, through my presentation. I completed my narrative by including some recommendations. At the end of it all, I asked my audience if they had any questions. There were a few questions. Then I asked the more senior people in the room if they had found my work valuable. Their answer humbled me.

They said, "You have pretty much validated everything we have known all along. Nothing new here. But thank you for your work anyway. And by the way, a lot of your recommendations will probably not work. We've already tried them."

And they had. Not because they had tried to follow some researcher's recommendations. As it turned out, I was the first real "researcher" to work with them. They had done their own research, and even though it might not have been as rigorous as the research I had done, they had learned a lot from things like following up on support tickets, running ad-hoc interviews with customers during conferences, and simply looking at what product features customers had welcomed over the years.

That was a huge lesson for me. In hindsight, I could have saved myself a lot of heartache if I had just asked those folks about what they already knew, and if I had involved them in making my recommendations. As it turned out, the meat of my research was disposed of very quickly as something that had already been done before! So hear me, and hear me well: you don't always have to do research just because you have some questions. Chances are, some people on your team are experienced. And they probably already know what you're going to tell them. Check with them first. And choose your research projects wisely. That is the only way people with experience will respect you.

Gut Feel

The brain makes decisions based on logic and emotions. Usually, emotions take center stage, although that fact is seldom acknowledged. Just because decisions are based on emotions, you shouldn't dismiss them as "unscientific." One of the main features that separate us humans from the rest of the animal kingdom is our ability to reason. And our ability to reason goes hand in hand with instinct or gut feel. When we don't have adequate data to make a decision, we rely on our ability to feel "in our gut."

And we use our gut feel way more than we give it credit for. In fact, psychologists argue that a lot of our cognition occurs outside the realm of our consciousness (5). Have you ever conducted a job interview? At the end of the interview, you need to make a decision on whether or not the candidate should be hired. How do you make your recommendation? If you think you are making a "hire" or a "no hire" recommendation based on sound, rational judgment, you are wrong, my friend! You are really making that recommendation based on how much you *liked* or *disliked* the candidate and your gut feel on how the candidate will perform once hired.

All the *rational* information you are collecting (like the candidate's resume, work experience, and performance during the interview) is merely being used to validate your assumptions about the candidate. You are really making the case for the candidate by using your instinct. And surprisingly, this often works! If you're in doubt, just look around you. Sure, some of your coworkers are jackasses, and you wonder how they got hired. But a good many of them are actually good employees and are even the right culture fit for the company. Many of them come in through employee recommendations (for which some companies pay a handsome amount). And recommendations are made purely by gut feel.

———

Chances are, people with experience already know what you're going to tell them.

The same holds true for some product decisions as well. It takes a bold product manager to go against conventional wisdom and assert that a new direction for the product will work. You can run user research on that feature and may even come back with findings that contradict the product manager's decision. But she goes with her decision just the same. You are pissed, but you don't have the power to oppose her decision. So you sit on the sidelines waiting for the feature to fail, but it doesn't. Her gut feel has worked. And it's because her instinct is not just a sort of funny feeling. Instinct often is grounded in real experience and wisdom. And the researcher needs to respect that.

Whoa! Does that mean you should never question any decision made by a product head based on pure instinct? No. No. No. That's not what I meant. All that I'm saying is—give a little bit of credit for instinct. Once in a while, let people make decisions based on gut feel, experience, or creative genius. You don't have to question every such decision or usability test the crap out of every decision. Pick your battles wisely.

So how do you know when going with gut feel is good and when it is not? What does it take to make that call? The answer is—experience. Your own experience. And you don't get that on your first day in the job. That takes some time. Until you feel you have honed your skills enough to decide what decision you should question and what you shouldn't, you should do what traditional researchers do—work with other experienced people to come to an informed decision.

2

I think, therefore I am...a researcher

Thinking like a researcher

On asking the right questions—

"What we observe is not nature itself, but nature exposed to our method of questioning."

—Werner Heisenberg

"Who questions much, shall learn much, and retain much."

—Francis Bacon

"Asking the right questions takes as much skill as giving the right answers."

—Robert Half

"Computers are useless. They can only give you answers."

—Pablo Picasso

"Judge a man by his questions rather than his answers."

—V<small>OLTAIRE</small>

And then there's this—

"I don't know if it's worth asking questions to which we already know the answers."

—VP <small>OF STRATEGY AND PLANNING TO A USER RESEARCHER</small>

There is a plethora of quotes out there on the importance of asking questions. And these quotes go back to so long ago that in some cases we don't even know who uttered the quote. We just satisfy ourselves with "old Chinese saying." So clearly, people have been on to something for hundreds, if not thousands of years.

Asking questions is vital. That's how we learn. That's how we used to learn as children. I know this for a fact. I used to be a child once. You ask a question because you are curious about something. It doesn't matter what you're curious about, or if the question can even be answered. Just asking a question guides the way you think and eventually expands your mind. Oddly enough, as our brains get more mature and we become more capable of comprehending complex concepts, the number of questions we ask falls rapidly. This is actually counterintuitive. As you get smarter, you should be asking more, not fewer questions! And there aren't many companies that actively encourage that. People are afraid of asking questions because there is a mistaken belief that asking too many questions is a sign of stupidity. And of course, people don't want to look stupid, even when they don't know the answers! We take a lot of things out there for granted, never bothering to question them.

———

Just asking a question guides the way you think and expands your mind.

Let me give you an example. I am going to deliberately talk about a situation that doesn't deal with user research, just to highlight the fact that pretty much every situation (and not just research) can do with some intelligent questioning. I used to work for a company where, while filing an expense report, it was mandatory to get managerial approval for any expense greater than $25. This was in a company where annual sales were in multiple billions of dollars. When I questioned the necessity for this practice, the answer was, "Unfortunately, there are cases where people have made false claims. So we actually want to use checks and balances in the approval process. It is a good accounting practice."

It may be good accounting practice. But what does it say about the culture of the company, and what does it say about the level of trust the company places on employees? If you suspect that your employee is attempting to bilk your company for amounts as small as $25 or $50, accounting checks and balances are probably not the issue here. Maybe you have bigger problems. Maybe you have trust issues with your employees and this is one of the ways it is getting manifested. Maybe you need to take a long, hard look at your corporate culture and hiring practices. Maybe you are not hiring people with integrity— or worse, people start compromising their integrity after joining your company!

The first step to fixing any problem is to recognize that the problem exists. And you do that by asking questions. "Why is the process so cumbersome? Why are there so many steps in the approval process? What would happen if we change the minimum approval amount to $100 instead of $25? What is the additional cost to the company in terms of increased approvals necessary for small expenses?" Asking questions provides an avenue for change. When you don't ask questions, you merely accept the status quo.

Also, there are two other things you need to bear in mind with regard to asking questions. The first is timing. A lot of questions lose their value if they are not asked at the right time. Take for instance a question like "Did I leave my stove on?" or "Is this shortness of breath and pain in my left arm indicative of a heart attack?" I don't know about you, but those kinds of questions are probably best asked as soon as possible. While not so time-sensitive, questions like "Who are the main stakeholders of this project?" or "What will success look like in this research study?" are also best asked sooner than later. The second thing you need to be aware of is that there is such a thing called *asking the right questions*. Just asking questions for the sake of asking them will not be of much help.

So what are these right questions that you need to be asking before commencing every research study? Always start every research project by asking, "Why am I doing this research?" I don't mean to ask this question at a philosophical level. We are not looking for answers like "We need research to make sure we are making the correct decision that will maxi-mize the value of our offerings to our customers. After all, we are in busi-ness because of them." While that kind of answer might move me to tears, it really doesn't add any real value to the problem at hand.

I mean this question quite literally. What I'm looking for is a verita-ble transformation of mindset. The question should broaden the mind. It should take the person who's asking the question from a fixed, closed mindset to an open mindset.

To understand this better, consider the following scenario. You are a researcher, and you are approached by Xander Xanaxx, manager of the support team. Xander is worried. For the past few quarters, the num-ber of customers raising support tickets has steadily decreased.[4] Xander feels it is probably because his team members are not doing their job well. He has also noticed that the average time to resolve a customer

---

4 In most companies, you can get customer support in more than one way. There's the company's website, which usually has a section devoted to documentation and trouble-shooting; then there's usually an 800 number you can call, although most companies are completely automating that and are trying to get away from even giving you a number in the first place. There's also a system by which you can actually log a customer support ticket. In some cases, you can log this by going on the company's website. In other cases, if you're dealing with a software company, you may be able to directly log this ticket from within the product itself.

issue has increased. Plus, the average complexity of support questions has increased, necessitating greater expertise on the part of the support agent resolving the issue. He wants to find out what really is happening and wants you to help him figure it out.

———

Always start every research project by asking, "Why am I doing this research?"

So, let's start with a list of necessary questions. We will begin by identifying the goal of the project. What is it? Is this goal commensurate with what Xander really wants to achieve? The project goal should not be "I need to interview ten customers." It should be more along the lines of "I need to determine why I'm even doing this research in the first place."

Note that I'm using the term "project goal" here. Project goals are different from research goals. A research goal is a subset of the overall project goal.

Xander's project is to improve his team's performance along a set of metrics. The research you are going to conduct for him is just a subset of what Xander wants to accomplish. It's a means to an end. Got it?

And why is the project goal important? If Xander achieves this goal, what problem is he solving? More importantly, does the goal even make sense from a strategic perspective?

Let's examine what will make Xander happy. As a manager, Xander wants his team to be more productive—to solve more customer issues than they did the previous quarter. In this case, his ideal situation is when his team reports that they have solved more customer issues this quarter. For this to happen, it is quite likely that the number of support tickets should increase. But what does it really mean when the number of support tickets increases? And is that even a good thing? Let's break this down into different possibilities and understand exactly what it means when the number of support tickets increases.

Possibility 1. The number of tickets could have increased because more customers have bought the product. This is actually a good thing for the company, and it's good for Xander too.

Possibility 2. The number of customers hasn't increased. But the number of issues they are reporting has. This could mean there is some sort of problem with the product. Maybe the latest version of the product has introduced some bugs. This is good for Xander but bad for his company.

Possibility 3. The number of customers hasn't increased, but the company has made it easier for customers to raise issues. Maybe they came up with a new way to log issues from within the product itself. Maybe they advertised their support more. Maybe they created a new form of phone support that customers find really easy to use. This is again good for the company and good for Xander, as there will eventually be more happy customers (assuming that the issues are solved, of course).

Similarly, we can break down Xander's request to understand the reason behind why the average time to resolve an issue has increased. Again, if Xander meets his goal (which is to decrease the average time to resolve an issue), it could imply one or a combination of the following.

Possibility 1. It could mean his team is taking a longer time to resolve simple and trivial issues. Maybe these issues are so simple that under normal circumstances a customer shouldn't even be bothering the support team by creating tickets. This is definitely bad for the company and for Xander.

Possibility 2. An increase in the resolution time could actually mean that the trivial issues are now being taken care of by some sort of automated process. For example, in the past customers could have bothered support every time they forgot their account password. But now the company has instituted an automated password-recovery system that takes care of the issue without using support overhead. This frees up the support agents to handle more complex problems, thereby increasing their response times. While this is a good for the company, Xander may not see it that way. In fact, he may be happier without the automated system!

This possibility also addresses Xander's third concern—that the average complexity of the issues may have increased. Xander is worried that he may have to train his existing staff more—or, worse, look for more competent agents. But this may actually be a good thing for the company and the customers.

As a researcher, you need to question whether what's good for the stakeholder is good for the whole company. In the case of support, things become especially tricky. It's like that in the medical profession too. For a doctor to become very busy and rich, she needs a lot of patients. But a lot of patients may mean there are more diseases overall, and an increase in people's health-care costs, and that's not good for society (well, this is the thinking in most parts of the world at least!).

As a researcher, you need to question whether what's good for the stakeholder is good for the whole company.

Coming back to Xander's case, we should even question the metrics Xander is using to evaluate his team's success. Do those same metrics determine the company's success as well? And what about the customer's success?

Take "time to resolve," for instance. Short resolution time could mean more efficient support staff and a reduction in the resolution cost per issue. That would be good for the company. But if it is occurring because there are more trivial issues that customers should really be solving themselves, then this is bad for the company (even if it makes Xander happy). You can do similar analysis of other metrics like issue severity, total number of issues, etc.

So the point I'm making here is to think through the goals clearly! Understand the implications of solving the problems. And make sure your stakeholder (Xander) understands those implications too. Oftentimes, conducting an exercise like this with the stakeholders before the project begins could result in re-stating the goals and priorities. Not doing this may put you on the path to solving the wrong problem. Not good.

So, getting back to formulating the goals:

The goal can be broken into two parts. The first part is to *understand why there has been a change in metrics.*

The second part of the goal is to understand whether the change in the metrics Xander mentioned even reflects a problem that Xander or the company should solve. In other words, *is there really a problem, and if so, why is it important to solve this problem?*

The question of why it is important to solve a given problem is one that I have seldom seen explicitly asked. Yet it is one of the most important questions a researcher should be asking. You see, a lot of the study requests that come to a researcher tend to be pretty shallow and not well thought out. Most people get caught up in their little problem and feel that any situation that confronts them can be solved with a bit of data. What they don't do is wonder whether the situation is actually a problem at all. Or maybe they are just looking at a symptom of a particular problem and confusing it with the problem itself.

Once we have understood exactly why we need to answer Xander's questions, we are logically driven to ask the next question: what will we do with the results? How will we use the data gathered by research? At this point, I would recommend a thought exercise: come up with different kinds of data that you might end up collecting. Try to formulate ideas on how you would use these different "flavors" of data. What will you do if the data agrees with your assumptions? What will you do if it doesn't? What will you do if the data suggests that you move in an entirely new direction? Do this exercise with the key stakeholders, and prepare them for anything you may discover.

What teams/divisions will be impacted by the research? This is another crucial question that explores the scope of the problem. What kind of task flows will be impacted? Who are the stakeholders whose buy-in you need? If the problem is limited to Xander's team, then yeah, his buy-in is enough. But it could reflect a larger problem with the product itself, or with the customer base. That would bring more stakeholders into the game.

And by "buy-in," I am not just referring to sponsorship. That's a given. What I'm really referring to is—who will act on the findings? If you come back with company-level recommendations, will the larger stakeholder community stand by you to act on them?

Different companies have different ways of dealing with this. In some companies (the ones that are a little more aware of why they are doing research), they usually commit resources to act on the findings even before the research is started. In others, the researcher needs to do research and come out with the findings. Then, based on what the findings indicate, stakeholders may decide to commit resources after the fact. But you have to have some sense beforehand of whether or not people will do something about the research. If you get the sense that no resources have been committed beforehand, and if you feel it is not terribly likely that resources will be committed even after you do the research, don't take up the project. You'll save yourself a lot of heartache.

What is the budget of the project? This is the obvious next question—closely tied to the sponsorship part of the buy-in. I have had two kinds of experiences here. In the first, the team that asked me to do research for them really had no intention of paying the project costs (including incentives to participants). They expected me to somehow cough up the money. Sure, I'll pay for the project, and while I'm at it, I'll also put all their children through college too!

The second set of experiences was more nuanced. In many companies, especially nontechnology companies, it is not uncommon for the team requesting research to take a pay-as-you-go approach. They expect the researcher to first run the study. Based on how valuable the findings are to them, the team will decide whether to pay for subsequent research projects. In such cases, I'd recommend that the researcher should take on the project. This is a good way to get a foot in the door. The researcher's own team should also have a budget just for such cases.

Asking the team the question about their budget will reveal the team's true intentions. Don't do the project without asking this question.

What are the key milestones in the project, and what is the timeline of the project? Another important question. You need to demonstrate progress in your work. Identifying milestones is a good way to do it.

What does success look like? Can you envision what will happen after you come back with the results and your findings are implemented? You should do this for multiple scenarios—whether the results are in your stakeholders' favor or contrary to what they are looking to accomplish.

How will you measure success? Are you using metrics to define your success? Are they along the lines of the same metrics that Xander is using?

If you figure out that those don't make sense, can you convince Xander to come up with new metrics that are good for his team, the company, and customers?

Once you figure all this out, you now move on to the second level of our goal-setting exercise: formulating the research goal (which, as I mentioned before, forms a subset of the project goals).

Research goal: Identify the causes for

1. The decrease in the number of support tickets
2. The increase in the average time to resolve a customer issue
3. The increase in the average complexity of support questions

And now, the meat of the research project: what research methods will you use to answer these questions? If had a dime for every time a product manager approached me with a method first without even detailing the research question he needed to answer…

In this context, I want to tell you something. If there's one thing you should take away from this book—well, I'm really hoping you take away more than one thing—but this one thing right here is very, very important, and I'm hoping you'll take it to heart. So remember this well: **Your question should always drive the research method. Never the other way around.**

Coming back to Xander's story, you already may have some quantitative metrics around support tickets, metrics like average time to resolve a customer issue and the complexity of support questions. Obviously. That's why Xander approached you in the first place. Now, in order to figure out why this happening, and what the extent of the problem is, you need to do some widespread quantitative research.

––––––

Your question should always drive the research method. Never the other way around.

The purpose of this research is twofold.

1. To see the extent of the problem. How widespread is it?
2. To see if Xander's information is accurate. Is the problem real? This second purpose is really optional; follow this thread only if you feel that Xander's data or his interpretation of the data might be suspect.

Now that you have a handle on the questions and the metrics you'd need to track, let's talk about the participants in your study. You'll have to work with two groups of people here—the support agents in your company who work on customer support tickets (even people who report to Xander) and your customers, the people who log these support tickets.

You need to do deep dives with your support agents to understand the delta—the changes they have noticed that are causing Xander his acidity. Then you'll have to work on how you'll get the answers from your customers. A simple survey with customers is recommended for this purpose. To set the survey up, you will, of course, need to ask a bunch of questions. I won't get into the actual survey questions here—that will be an unnecessary distraction from the main thesis of this section.

By now, I think I have given you the hang of what I'm trying to say. In order to be successful as a researcher, you need to ask a lot of questions. At different levels. Some questions could be aimed at the team members you're working with. Others could be aimed at a much broader level of stakeholders, sometimes even the top executives of the company itself. A lot of the questions don't even have anything to do with what you'd be asking participants of a research study. These are questions that you'd be asking internally, within your company. And these are important because they serve to validate or invalidate the study hypothesis. And there's that word again—hypothesis.

3

How I learned to stop worrying and love the hypothesis[5]

Formulating a hypothesis

"My hypothesis is that people will really like these designs."
And "Shouldn't we clarify our hypothesis before we begin our design spike?"

—A UX RESEARCHER WHO USES THE WORD *HYPOTHESIS* WHENEVER HE MEANS *THOUGHT, ASSUMPTION,* OR *QUESTION*. HE ALSO USES HYPOTHESIS AS ITS OWN PLURAL.

This is one of my pet peeves. People (researchers and nonresearchers alike) use the word *hypothesis* with aplomb. The problem is, most of these people don't seem to have a clue what it means, or even when they should use it. It is one thing when the average employee does it. It is a bit more troubling when a researcher does it. It has bothered me so much, I'm going to devote a whole chapter to it.

---

5 Note to the worried: This chapter doesn't contain math or formulas. The intent here is to build a good hypothesis without getting too technical about it.

What is a hypothesis? How can a researcher use it as part of scientific inquiry? And when should a hypothesis be used?

A big part of research actually focuses on inferring the relationship between two variables. For the sake of illustration, let's consider the following statement: *Increasing product discount will lead to a higher NPS value for the product.*

NPS, as you may well know, stands for *net promoter score*. It is typically measured as a response to the question "How likely is it that you would recommend <the product or company> to a friend or colleague?" on an 11-point scale (from 0 to 10). When a participant gives a score of 9 or 10, she is considered a *promoter*.

———

A big part of research actually focuses on inferring the relationship between two variables.

If she gives 7 or 8, she is said to be *passive.* Anything lower, and she is a *detractor* (6). You obtain the NPS score by subtracting the percentage of detractors from the percentage of promoters[6]. Obviously, you want a high NPS score.

Now, given two variables (in our case: product discount and NPS), we wish to assess whether a causal relationship exists between the variables. In other words, if the discount on a product is increased (or decreased), does it respectively increase (or decrease) the NPS for the product?

When you undertake a research study, you do so with some idea of what outcomes to expect. The relationship between the discount and number of customers can be predicted by an experimental hypothesis (7).

———

6 The highest possible NPS is 100, which means that there are no detractors, and all the respondents are promoters. The lowest of course, is -100, which implies that every single respondent is a detractor. That can't be good for any company!

So, what is a hypothesis?

A hypothesis is a claim. You want to test whether this claim is true or false.

The claim is typically made about a population. As it is usually not possible to test the entire population, researchers tend to test the claim on a *sample* of the population. The key here is that you need to pick out exactly what you're making the claim about. In other words, what exactly do you want to test?

Let's assume that right now the NPS value for the product is 5. As it turns out, 5 is not very high as NPS values go. While most companies keep their NPS scores a closely guarded secret, there are independent groups that publish NPS for specific companies and industries. According to one such source (8), Tesla enjoys an NPS of 97. Costco has a 45. Southwest Airlines has an NPS of 62. On the other hand, a score of 5 is not very bad either. Quite a few companies have a negative NPS as well. (A negative NPS means that the product has more detractors than promoters.)

So you want to see if offering a discount on the product moves that NPS value. Given two variables (discount and number of customers), one of two outcomes is possible. There is either a relationship between the two variables or there isn't. Manipulating the discount will either increase or decrease the NPS, or it won't. A hypothesis describes the predicted outcome you may or may not find in a research study.

I could get really technical here by talking about things like alternative hypothesis and null hypothesis. But I realized I don't need to get that detailed. Most research done in companies does not need that level of sophistication when it comes to formulating and testing hypotheses. Instead, I am going to show you how to evolve a testable hypothesis without throwing in too much math.

But before I begin formulating hypotheses, think about this: Why is it even important to come up with a hypothesis? In what way does that help with research or product development?

Gather around, children, for here's the answer:

First off, you base your understanding of the world around you by asserting some facts, such as: it is warmer in the sun than in the shade, pizzas are the tastiest things on earth, etc.

A hypothesis is nothing but that—a statement. But you don't know whether the statement (or claim) is a fact or not. If you are going to base your strategy/product on it, then you need to be sure the claim is true. Second, all claims are based on some underlying truths. You need to be explicit about the truth behind the claim, as that is what affects your understanding of the claim. Third, clearly formulating hypotheses gives you an opportunity to test them. Without hypotheses, your assumptions will be just that—assumptions. Make sense?

Before we resume with the NPS example, let's do another, simpler one. This time, let's see how we can come up with a testable hypothesis from scratch. To do that, let's come up with a situation that would warrant some hypothesis testing.

Amy, an employee of a commuter train company, notices that the trains tend to be less crowded during summer months. She believes this is because more people tend to take vacations during summer when the temperatures are warmer.

She comes up with a rough hypothesis:

Temperature affects the number of people who travel by train.

This is a good start. It has identified all the key things she'd need to test. But things are a bit ambiguous. For instance, "temperature" is pretty general, and it doesn't really talk about what she has assumed to be a main cause: summer months. The word "affects" is also pretty ambiguous, because it doesn't really talk about what kind of impact is had by summer months. Amy should refine this hypothesis so it become easier to test.

Commuters tend to travel less by train during summer months.

This narrows things down a bit more. First, she narrowed "people" to "commuters." That's the group Amy wanted to test anyway. "Temperature" has been refined to "summer months." It's easier to define and measure what she means by summer months. But can she do even better? Probably. She can definitely do better than using phrases like "tend to." So Amy refines this hypothesis a little more:

Commuters travel less by train during summer because they go on vacations.

So what did she do here? For starters, she removed the ambiguity introduced by "tend to." Next, she defined clear, measurable variables. Travel can be measured by the presence or absence of a commuter on a given day. Summer months can be clearly defined as the time period between June Solstice and September Equinox. There is also a possible causal factor thrown in—vacations, which can be clearly defined. By doing this, Amy can actually see if there is a correlation between summer months and the attendance of commuters, and if that is caused by commuters going on vacation. Amy decides her hypothesis is in a good place and she can stop refining it. Now that she's got this hypothesis, she can turn it into a sort of a template.

When doing this on your own, I recommend that you word the hypothesis in the following manner:

I believe that < state your belief >
because <state the causal factor>.

Example:

I believe that commuters travel less by train during summer months because they go on vacations.

In this template, the hypothesis has two components. The first component states the claim, and the second component states the causal factor that could be contributing to the claim. In this format, you get to clearly state both, so that it becomes easier to test the hypothesis and verify whether the thing you've identified as a causal factor does indeed cause the claim to be true.[7] Now that you have the format down, you are ready to test the hypothesis.

Hypothesis testing

In a nutshell, here's what you do. You test the claim. You also test the proposed causal factor that you mentioned (which forms the foundation of your hypothesis).

For illustration, let's use the hypothesis we've been building.

Commuters travel less by train during summer because they go on vacations.

You want to assess what you mean by "travel less," and therein, you run into a problem. You can't really calculate the number of commuters in every single train. That would be too hard and impractical. The solution would be to get a sample at a given time slot—say, the average number of commuters who travel during a certain time of day between two

---

7 Note that in some cases, the claim could be true, but what you've identified as the underlying causal factor could be false.

predefined train stations (that represent two typical stations). That's easier to measure. But you should come up with a representative sample. Let's say you are able to come up with just such a sample with Amy's help. And, for now, let's assume that the sample you come up with is perfectly representative.

Let's now look at the number of commuters who travel in the nonsummer months. You need to use this as a reference. Let's say that between the hours of 8:00–9:30 a.m. (rush hour), an average of six thousand passengers take the train every weekday between train stations A and B[8] between the September Solstice and the June Equinox (nonsummer months).

To test the hypothesis, you need to prove that during summer months, this average value *is less than* six thousand.

You need one more thing to test the hypothesis. It's called a test statistic. A test statistic is calculated from some sample data. This helps you determine if the data on hand is statistically significant enough to accept the hypothesis.

And what do I mean by statistically significant? Statistical significance is a term that indicates where to draw the line that will help you decide whether or not to accept your hypothesis.

So, shall we start looking at test statistics and do some actual hypothesis testing? Actually, we aren't going to do that. That takes us too deep into the realm of statistics, and that isn't the goal of this chapter. The goal

---

8 In reality, there are many things you'd need to consider. For instance, you may not need to actually count the number of people traveling between two stations (commonly called "ridership"). Most commuter train companies already have these numbers on hand. They usually calculate things like daily ridership, rush-hour ridership, and ridership between different stations. You could choose stations from a predominantly residential area to the most crowded downtown area of the city and look up the ridership numbers during morning and evening rush hours. Most train companies also have predefined rush hours, so you may not need to reinvent that wheel either. If you're lucky, they may have defined summer just the way you have defined it here, or they could go by school holidays in that region—which, if you think about it, lends more credibility to the vacation hypothesis; people tend to take vacations centered more around their children's school schedules than by when the June Solstice or September Equinox occurs!

of this chapter is to tell you what a hypothesis should look like in order to serve as a valid starting point of your research.

But, at the same time, I don't want to leave you hanging. There's a reason why I am talking about hypotheses, and I'm going to wrap this chapter up by reinforcing some concepts regarding hypothesis formulation.

First off, not every English sentence or question is a hypothesis. A hypothesis should be a claim that explores a causal relationship. Second, you need to make sure the hypothesis is grounded in some sort of real-world situation or background study. In the first instance, above, we started with an NPS value of 5. This was the initial value of NPS that corresponded to a "no discount" scenario. What surprises me is that in most real-world situations, many people don't even start with this initial scenario.

Finally, in order to be considered a good researcher who knows his stuff, you really need to internalize the concept of hypothesis and how it should be tested. It's not too hard once you get the hang of it. You should hone the skill of taking any situation and coming up with a testable hypothesis. You don't have to do this when you do usability testing. But you're not just a usability tester. You are a researcher, and you need to understand causation. You need to help others understand causation—and hypothesis testing is a crucial part of that.

———

A hypothesis is a claim that explores a causal relationship.

Now let's get back to the original NPS example. In this case, the hypotheses could be stated as:

I believe offering discounts will increase the NPS of the product because people tend to promote products that have a greater value for money.

To wrap this chapter up, here are few common situations that lend themselves to hypothesis testing. Examine the way these sentences are phrased. Then see if you can formulate hypotheses from them. I've deliberately not provided the supporting factual statements in some cases, because in real life, not every claim comes with such statements. Feel free to come up with your own facts.

    a. Using solar panels on roofs will reduce the cost of your power consumption (you can add a fact here that hasn't been defined explicitly, like *"because you believe that solar energy is cheaper than conventional energy"*).

    b. Cigarettes cause cancer (again, you can add a factual bit at the end of each of the following).

    c. People with college degrees earn more money than people with just high-school diplomas.

    d. People driver faster at night than during the day.

    e. People who read this book will achieve greater success as researchers than people who don't. (This one doesn't need to be tested. It's already proven to be true!)[9]

Now that we went over "hypothesis," let's look at the other insanely maligned word in research—"insights."

---

9 Here are some hypotheses you could come up with for the first 4 scenarios:

    a. I believe that using solar panels on roofs will reduce the cost of power consumption because solar energy is cheaper than conventional energy.

    b. I believe that cigarettes cause cancer because they contain a lot of carcinogens.

    c. I believe that people with college degrees earn more money than people with just high-school diplomas because people with college degrees tend to get higher-paying jobs.

    d. I believe that people drive faster at night than during the day because the darkness of the night hides roadside distractions.

4

All work and no insight makes you a dull researcher

Coming up with insights

"I can create the proposal, build a screener document, schedule participants, run research sessions, analyze the results, and prepare a really good report. The only thing I don't know is how to generate insights!" (followed by a nervous chuckle)

—USER RESEARCHER DURING A PERFORMANCE REVIEW

The word "insight" is one of the most maligned and bastardized words in recent times. And the research community is partly to blame for this. You see, in order to make themselves seem more important, researchers have started to claim that pretty much every finding in a research study is an insight. Almost every study I encounter has a section titled "insights." That's right. Insights. In the plural form. As if insights are so common that every study, even a usability test yields multiple insights. I have often been asked, "What are your insights from your latest study?" In response, I tell them what I found—just observations and inferences, nothing more. And sadly, people are satisfied with the answers I give if I call them insights.

Does this mean that no study can have insights? Or that it is impossible for a usability study to yield insights—that somehow only specific kinds of studies are insight worthy? And how can one even come up with an insight? In order to answer these questions, it is really important to understand exactly what an insight is. When you do, you'll also understand that the questions above don't even make sense. You've been thinking about them all wrong. Very meta, isn't it?

The Cambridge dictionary defines an insight as "a clear, deep, and sometimes sudden understanding of a complicated problem or situation, or the ability to have such an understanding" (9). This implies that an insight is some sort of an ability or capacity. Merriam-Webster dictionary defines insight as "the act or result of apprehending the inner nature of things or of seeing intuitively" (10). The Free Dictionary (I'll stop referring to dictionaries after this—I promise) defines the word as "the ability to discern the true nature of a situation, especially by intuition" (11). Why do I keep referring to dictionaries? Because I was amazed that they define insight with words like "sudden understanding" and "intuition." Particularly "intuition."

The key to understanding what an insight is rests in this one word: intuition. Now, what does intuition mean? I'm not going to start quoting from dictionaries again; you already know I'm capable of it. Instead, I'm going to give you the most pertinent definition straight up, after looking up various sources (actually I used the same sources I did for "insight"). Intuition is the ability to understand something without needing to think about it, or without using reason to discover it. Synonyms of intuition include clairvoyance, premonition, and sixth sense. Wow! So unscientific!

So here we are. We are researchers. Scientists. We ask sharp, meaningful questions. We formulate hypotheses. We identify the right method tailored to answering the research question. We conduct tests rigorously, taking every care to avoid biases. Then we meticulously document all our findings and conduct thorough, detailed analysis. And all for what—to get insights that are derived from intuition? All that science…is it just an eyewash? Are researchers nothing more than glorified diviners? WTF?

Well, if you are thinking such thoughts, let us break down this whole "insight" thing by coming up with a working definition for that word.

Here it is: *An insight is an intuitive leap that reveals a truth.*

There really isn't a set path to get there. That's important to keep in mind. Also, what does an insight look like? How do you know when you have had an insight? What kinds of symptoms does an insight generate? In truth, there is no way to clearly identify when you've had an insight. When you have an insight, you just have an insight. You just do. It just makes sense. Can you prove that an insight is true? Sometimes yes, and sometimes no. In some cases, you can translate an insight into a hypothesis directly, and you can set up experiments in which you can prove whether the hypothesis is valid or not. In other cases, you can only prove the existence of behaviors that are possibly a result of the insight being true.

Of course, you need to be very careful here and not confuse correlation with causality. Also, in such cases, you need to realize that you are merely proving that the underlying facts you've collected are true; you are not really proving the truth of the insight itself. That's the deal with psychology. A field like psychology is not what you'd call an exact science. It's not like math or physics. Psychology deals with things that go on within the human mind, but all these things become relevant to us only if they are manifested in some sort of behavior. (In fact, the American Psychological Association defines "psychology" as the study of mind *and behavior* (12).) And human behavior is arbitrary. It is unpredictable, and is incredibly hard to aggregate. Worst of all, behavior is not easy to quantify.

An insight is an intuitive leap that reveals the truth.

But the underlying motivations for behavior do reveal themselves once in a while. And that's what you are really going after when you do research. You are trying to understand what is causing an observable behavior.

Getting to the root cause is tricky, and the path to discovery is plagued by things like biases, incorrect hypotheses, and application of wrong methods. That's what researchers are constantly trying to avoid.

So, when can you actually get an insight? How much work needs to be done before you uncover an insight? To understand the mechanisms behind insight generation, and how you can validate the truth of an insight, let's look at an example.

I was asked to prepare the persona of a chief marketing officer. My company was coming up with a dashboard targeted at marketing executives, because if there is one thing in the world a top-level marketer needs, it's one more dashboard. In order to build the dashboard, my company's sales team figured that they needed to understand said executives a bit deeper before trying to sell stuff to them.

One of the target users of this dashboard was the highest executive in the world of marketing, the CMO. I was commissioned to build the persona of one. My company even funded me to hire an external agency to help dig up data for the persona. We started by collecting information about CMOs from any source we could find (the low-hanging fruit obviously was to start looking at their LinkedIn profiles). I learned about the kind of schools they went to. From Facebook, we found out where they hang out, where they vacation, and what they do when they are not working (which is a very small part of their lives). We learned about where they get their information and what kinds of magazines they like to read (*The Economist* figured on top of that list).

We then ran a bunch of interviews with them (or with the CMOs who could carve out some time to talk to us; they were not enticed by the incentives we usually pay our users, like the average participant in a user research study). We learned about their motivations and professional aspirations (a lot of them wanted to be CEOs). We learned about their work habits and the kind of tools they use. And finally, we learned about their business needs—what kind of information they were looking for that would make them successful in their jobs. I took all this information, synthesized it, and built the CMO's persona.

Armed with all this knowledge, we set about building some concepts for the product we were building for them. We tested them, iterated on them, and refined them. More testing followed. We finally came up with what we thought was the winning concept. It evolved into a prototype. We tested it for usability. As the product went into production, we realized we needed to come with an effective strategy to actually sell this to CMOs.

Now here's the thing—a lot of companies try to sell a lot of stuff to marketing executives. And here's another thing—tons of companies make dashboards for marketing executives. So we really needed to stand out. We had done a lot of hard work in understanding the user persona. The research was solid. The persona was well fleshed out[10]. The design was well thought out and was based on customer feedback. We even did iterative development of the designs. We had crossed all the t's and dotted all the i's.

But when we tried to come up with a sales strategy, we quickly discovered that our product couldn't stand out all by itself. This was clearly not a case of "if you build it, they will come."[11] We needed to do something more. We needed to reach our target market at a visceral level. And that's where we were falling short. Our CMO persona was still missing that crucial thing—that one thing that would reach into the CMO's psyche and tug at their heartstrings. A few quick walkthroughs with CMOs, and I realized I had to go back to the drawing board.

I started looking at the data. I was missing something. I went over all the data points again, looking for clues like a forensic detective looks for that one piece of damning evidence. And then I found it. The secret was in the tenure of the CMO. I discovered that the average tenure of the CMO was less than four years. In recent times, it has fallen even more (13).

---

10 Most people tend to say "flushed out" instead of "fleshed out". To flesh something out is to give it substance, like adding flesh to a skeleton. To "flush out" is to bring something out of its hiding place, like flushing out a raccoon from its lair in your attic.

11 Attributed to the movie *Field of Dreams*. The actual quote is "If you build it, *he* will come". Most people remember it as "…*they* will come". A classic case of the Mandela effect (a term used to describe collective misremembrance).

For the size of the company I was interested in, the average tenure of the CMO was eighteen months. That was it. Just eighteen months. That put everything else into perspective. All the information they were gathering. All the information they were looking for. It all made sense now! This was the "aha" moment I was desperately looking for!

The CMOs were driven by one emotion. Fear. Fear of losing their jobs. This paranoia was underneath all their actions. Everything they did was to make sure they impressed the people at the top of the company so they could stay employed.

Now let's say my team found a way to appeal to that fear—a way to demonstrate to the CMO that our dashboard would keep them on top of everything they needed to know at all times. Information is power, and we wanted to give the CMO the right kind of information at the right time in digestible chunks through our dashboard. That's a powerful thing, right?

Long story short, we ended up creating a sales strategy around that idea, that *insight*. Remember—the insight I'm talking about is not the fact that the tenure is short. That is data. The insight is the fact that the low tenure leads to extreme fear, and that fear is the driving force behind everything they do. I am going to stop this story right here, as the rest of it is not relevant to the point I'm making.

There you have it. Insight. How did this insight arise? What's the process here? Now remember, there are a lot of books that deal with analysis. But not many of them talk about how to synthesize an insight during that analysis. So I'm going to outline a simple framework for generating an insight with four crucial steps: Collecting, Slicing, Digging Deep, and Processing.

COLLECTING

You start by collecting facts. All the facts you can collect. You need to remember that there are two basic kinds of facts, which are reflected in two basic kinds of data. There is numeric data, fondly called quantitative data by researchers. Broadly speaking, numeric data tells you what's going on. Such data can be very insightful in and of itself. But there's another kind of data, qualitative data, that explains the psychographics behind the numbers. Psychographics refers to things like behaviors, aspirations, attitudes...all the good stuff that goes into influencing how people think and makes them do the things they do. Psychographic data explains the how and the why behind the numbers.

To make an insight complete, meaningful, and—most importantly— actionable, you need to package the truth revealed by numbers with the wisdom of psychographics.

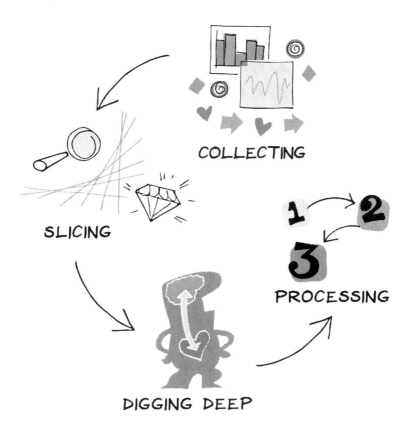

COLLECTING

SLICING

PROCESSING

DIGGING DEEP

For example, with quantitative data you may be able to get the information that parents of only children tend to buy more gifts for their children. This information, by itself, is quite useful, especially if you're in the business of marketing toys. But let's say you supplement this data with data gathered from interviews (qualitative data). Let's say you are able to infer that the real reason this happens is because only children are more common in urban areas, and most of these children are actually latchkey kids, because both the parents have to work to pay their bills, and a lot of these parents feel guilty that they are not spending enough time with their children, and this guilt is manifested in the form of toys they buy their kids. Boom! Now that's an insight! Such an insight can be used not only in targeting the parents of only children with clever marketing strategies, but also in product development itself. Toys made for these latchkey kids can incorporate elements that combat the loneliness the kids possibly face. They can also be designed to let parents and kids play together. You can come up with a myriad of ideas, all as a result of just one critical insight.

Now that you've completed data collection of all kinds, you begin the process of making sense of the data. You start by...

SLICING

There is more than one way to skin a cat. There are similar proverbs with regard to killing dogs too. Some of these originated more than three hundred years ago (14). Now, why anyone would want to kill dogs and skin cats is beyond me. But the intent of these proverbs is important to keep in mind. There are many ways to do something. And if there is one field where this is extremely pronounced, it's data analysis.

An insight is like a diamond in the rough. If you don't remove the "rough" surrounding it in just the right way, the diamond that's hiding inside will lose its luster, and therefore its value. It all comes down to how you slice it.

And it works the same way with data too. There are many ways to slice your data set. But it's only the right cut of data that will reveal the insight in all its glory.

How do you know what the right slice is? You don't. No one does. It's unique to each data set and the question you are seeking to answer. But you, as a researcher, have something that others don't. Like a diamond cutter, you know two things. You can't rest until you've explored every possible slice that you can. And you have a sense for what slice of data would yield the most powerful insight. You have this sense because you are capable of formulating meaningful hypotheses, and because you have experience doing this kind of thing.

Slicing is, in essence, an exploratory technique. It's the part of data analysis that will lead you to unexplored territory. When you take this journey, you may end up with an insight that you never knew existed—or you may not. But you won't know that until you slice the data every which way possible.

Example: product churn (attrition) could be caused by cost of the product, the way the product performs, the customer support offered by the company, the lack of features that the customers require, or a combination of one or more of these variables. The smart researcher would collect as much data as possible and try to examine if changes in one variable are causing changes in the final outcome (churn) or in other variables. Each slice of data needs to be examined carefully. Maybe it's just price. Maybe it's a combination of customer support and product performance. But you won't know that until you have the right slices of data.

There are many ways to slice your data. But it's the right cut of data that will reveal the insight in all its glory.

DIGGING DEEP

In my chapter on the touchy-feely things (chapter 7), I talk about emotions and the psychographic aspect of things. At the risk of stealing my own thunder, I'm going to talk a little bit about it here too.

Your insights are deepest only when you understand the psychology behind them. And that means getting down into what really causes behavior to manifest—the motivations, the aspirations, and the core thinking patterns. This is where you are very likely to get into the irrational side of things. Be ready for this. Human beings are irrational for the most part. But this side rarely shows up during the initial state of exploration of causal factors. During the initial stages, you are always confronted with rationality. But if you keep persisting, you get beyond the façade and get into the real, crazy, irrational world, the human world.

"Wait!" you scream. "People may make irrational decisions in the consumer world. But not in the enterprise world. Not in the business world." Yeah, no, that's not entirely true. Even in the so-called business world, it's really human beings who make decisions. And I might argue, it is really one human being who ultimately drives that decision. And even if the decision is influenced by a bunch of influencers, they are human too. Which makes them fundamentally prone to emotional decisions…irrational decisions. Decisions like "I didn't hire that person because he didn't stand up when he shook my hand" (true story) or "Google does it. Amazon does it. That's the way we should go" (one designer to another at a company I worked for).

And that's the kind of stuff you should uncover when you say you're uncovering insights. You need to answer the following:

What behavior determines important outcomes (the ones you desire, and the ones you don't)?

When does the behavior occur?

What is common among the people who display that behavior?

Who is responsible for this behavior?

What is the result of the behavior?

What reinforces the behavior?

What are the common behavioral patterns?

Finally, can you leverage this behavior, or do you need to modify it? If you have to modify behavior, how do you go about it?

PROCESSING

At its heart, processing is the step of data analysis where you tie your analysis back to the goal of your project. This is where you find out if all the data you've collected is actually telling you a story. Processing may often occur in tandem with Digging Deep. It's hard to tease them apart sometimes. But this dimension of thinking is essential to close the research loop.

This is also the stage where you assess if you have collected enough data, and if the type of data you've collected is adequate to tell the story you wish to tell. You may need to conduct one more rounds of data collection to answer those questions.

When you are busy trying to tease out the emotional bits, you may discover that you need to answer a whole new set of questions—questions that you had not even thought about when you started out with data collection. You know what this means, don't you? It means you may have to do another round of data collection (or maybe even two rounds!).

Most researchers dread this moment. They believe it is a sign of weakness. And so do a lot of people who work with researchers, either in the capacity of peers or even managers. A lot of people don't understand that in order to get to the core of something, they have to embark on a journey of discovery. And when you're on such a journey, the complete path is seldom visible at the very outset. It is only when you've completed a part of the journey that more and more intricacies start revealing themselves. This could mean that research could be drawn out and may cost more money than initially budgeted. This could also mean that the researcher has to say "I don't know yet" for a little while longer.

———

In order to get to the core of something, you have to embark on a journey of discovery where the path ahead of you is not clearly visible. You may need to do more research that you initially anticipated.

Unfortunately for the researcher, this is one stage when things start to break down. The product/design team is often unwilling to wait a little longer, and they start making decisions without the benefit of research insights. This is also the stage when the researcher needs to communicate that he hasn't failed. He has in fact started to synthesize what could be some pretty meaningful stuff. But all this is possible only if people around the researcher are a little more patient and place a little more trust in the researcher. Easier said than done, right?

How does the effective researcher manage this stage? Well, first off, the researcher needs to ask himself this: given the nature of the research question he is trying to answer, how long could it possibly take to complete the research and analysis? The more unclear the question, or the broader the question, the more involved the research is going to be, and the more rat holes the researcher is going to be lured into.

Then the researcher needs to set expectations for his team. He should use some relevant past studies he has conducted as examples showing what these journeys look like, what they may cost, and how long they may take.

The researcher also needs to keep the team constantly updated on the progress of the analysis work. He has been good so far about involving stakeholders in the data-collection stage. Now he should keep them informed about the different milestones in the analysis. He should tell them what he has uncovered and what other questions have sprung up that may need to be answered in order to compose the whole story.

Finally, he needs to anticipate the stakeholders' schedules and deadlines. Even if he comes up with some earth-shattering insights, they will be useless if not revealed to the stakeholders on time. This calls for some pretty intensive project planning on the researcher's part, but it's got to be done. Otherwise, all his efforts are wasted.

And by the way, working with a team helps. One important thing with this whole insight-generating plan is that you really don't have to work alone. I understand that sometimes you need to work alone and do some deep thinking to come up with insights. But from my own experience, and from watching some really smart people who came up with incredible insights, I discovered that, for the most part, this need not be a journey you undertake alone. Take some people along on your journey. They may help in many ways. For instance, they may ask questions that you haven't asked (and you know how important that can be). They may view things from a different perspective. They may slice the data in ways you hadn't thought of. They may interpret and process data in a completely different way. The list goes on.

"Hold on!" you say. "This is my research project. Insight generation is the most crucial part of any research. You want me to hand that over to others? What about me? How can I assert my importance? And what qualifies those people to generate insights? Isn't insight generation a researcher's prerogative?"

All valid questions, my friend. I am going to address them in the form of a fun FAQ section, right here!

Fun FAQs about including people in generating insights

1. How can I assert my importance as a researcher if I let others participate in insight generation?

Funny you should ask. Here's something I discovered when I involved people in insight generation—*they ended up respecting me more!* A lot of times, people just want to feel included. They don't like it when a researcher (or anyone else, for that matter) disappears for a few days and reappears with a to-do list for the whole team. Two things happen when you include people in insight generation. First, they get to see your process first hand. They understand that you are methodical and rigorous and there is method to your seeming madness. They see that you are no longer the quack they thought you were! And second, they get to have their voices heard. They have ideas too, and some of them may be good ones. If you take their smart ideas into consideration, they will be more open to listening to *your* smart ideas. I believe it's called *quid pro quo*. So share more, and you will only get richer! Whoo-hoo! That's so meta I gave myself goosebumps!

2. But won't they try to take control? Won't they impose their will on the ideas being generated?

Well, let me tell you a little secret. If a product manager wants to take over and ignore your process, *he is going to do it anyway!* Just because you invited him to your analysis workshop doesn't change the situation in any way. You're going to have to deal with him sometime during your journey. Might as well be now, in front of a whole bunch of people. That way, others will at least get to see what is really going on.

If a product manager wants to take over and ignore your process, he is going to do it anyway!

3. I am the resident expert in research. What qualifies others to generate insights with me?

This question can be reworded as "what qualifies people to generate insights?" The answer is: they must be capable of reasoning. This is the same as saying they must be human beings. Seriously. That's all. Anyone can generate insights. Anyone. When I conduct a research-analysis workshop, I often invite people from outside the core product area—people who may be only remotely connected with the product. I have discovered that these people are so far away from the product they come without bias. They also present some very interesting perspectives that people who are close to the product can never think of.

4. In what other way is working with people beneficial?

Well, let's see…There is that loneliness thing that researches sometime face. You know, when you are the only researcher in the team, and everybody else belongs to a different team? Guess what—they now know you exist. They also know that you have some skills that they probably don't. Where does all this lead? They just might invite you to that next happy hour! If that isn't a good reason to include people, I don't know what is.

5

Do you smell what I'm steppin' in?

Translating insights into product design

"How do you actually take the insights from a research study and include them in your designs?"

—QUESTION FROM A DESIGN INTERN ON HER FIRST DAY ON THE JOB

"We let our designers figure that out. Ha! Ha! Ha!"

—HER MANAGER'S ANSWER

In the previous chapter, we saw how to come up with actionable insights. We learned that there isn't one set path for generating an insight. We also learned that sometimes we may not learn anything worth being considered an insight. That's OK. We don't have to feel depressed about it.[12] There will always be more studies in the future, and with them, more opportunities for generating insights.

---

12 Sometimes, not getting anything significant is an insight in itself, a fact that, I have found, is often lost on researchers. Added to this is another fact: you don't look cool declaring, "I found nothing of significance"!

52

Now comes the toughest part. What should you do with all those insights? You can just lob the insights over the wall and hope someone will pick them up and run with them. Insights, even actionable ones, are still pretty hard to parse into a language that designers or product managers understand. But unless you do this, unless you take this crucial step in making the implication of the insight easy to understand, all the work you've done so far is pretty damn useless. In order to make the insight actionable, you need to follow a clear process where you map the insight to the problem you're trying to solve. Let me illustrate why this step is important. I'm going to digress again, but by now you should be used to it.

When my kids were in middle school (junior high), we used to attend open houses at their school. An open house was one of the few opportunities we'd get to speak with their teachers face to face. During one such conversation with their math teacher, I asked, "So, Mrs. Numbermeister, what's the biggest challenge you face in teaching math to middle-schoolers?" I was expecting her to say something along the lines of "getting them to focus" or "making them get interested in math." Instead, she said, "Getting them to show their work!" "Huh," I said. "Why is it so important for them to show their work? Isn't it enough if they get the right answer?" To which she said something that at that time didn't seem important but in hindsight made a lot of sense. "As it turns out," she said, "a lot of kids don't exactly understand the value of each step in getting to that final solution. Quite often, the solution seems evident, but they can't articulate how they got there. If they don't understand the process, they may not be able to repeat their success with each problem."

Think about it. Even when the solution to the problem is sometimes very obvious, unless you understand the steps involved in the process, it is going to be hard to replicate the method.

It's the same story with insights. Sometimes, clever designers know exactly what to do with a given insight. They are immediately and intuitively able to come up with exactly the design solution the doctor ordered. But if you ask them to spell out what the thinking process was, they're at a loss. This makes it difficult to a) replicate the process with another insight

53

and b) teach other designers and product managers how they arrived at the solution.

And that's where this chapter comes in. I am going to share a method that Ben (the illustrator of this book) and I have used successfully ourselves. By no means is this the only method to come up with a design solution from insights. But like I said, it has worked for us and we thought we should share it with you. So here goes: let's unravel the mystery behind translating insights into design decisions.

Let's start with a relatively simple example. Sarah is a user researcher. She works for a company that makes a project-management application called Projection. The main sales channel of the product is the company's website. The company follows a freemium model. Interested users simply register themselves on the website and can try Projection free for one month. If the users like the product, they can continue using it by signing up for one of three different payment plans—Personal, Business, and Premium. Each plan offers different structures and features. Premium is meant for enterprise customers. Business is for small businesses, and Personal, of course, is the light version for individuals.

> If you don't understand the process you use to get to the solution, you may not be able to repeat your success with each problem.

The product is pretty good, and with just a little marketing, it seems to hold its own against much more established products in the market. However, not everything is perfect in the world of Projection. The company's data-analysis team has come up with a troubling finding: for some reason, almost 50 percent of the people who sign up to try the product don't seem to stick around. They seem to get as far as the first setup screen and then drop off right away.

Sarah has been entrusted with the task of determining what exactly is going on. She dutifully conducts a couple of research studies and comes back with a crucial insight. She has worked on refining the insight so that it is clear to understand and actionable. Here's her insight:

Many people who try Projection the first time don't stick around because there is not really enough content on there to engage with; they're not clear on what their next step should be. They really want the software to tell them what to do next.

As insights go, that's a fairly straightforward one (I'm also deliberately presenting a simple one so that I can demonstrate the process of translating this insight into design).

And that is **Step 1** in the process of translating an insight into design. Make sure the insight is crisp. Clear to understand. And actionable.

Step 2. Break that insight down. Work up a range of hypotheses based on that insight.[13]

We'll start by creating two hypotheses from the insight above. Two hypotheses because, if you observe carefully, there are two things that contribute to people dropping off—not enough content, and a lack of clarity on what to do next.[14]

Hypothesis 1:
We believe that instead of just presenting the users with empty space, including some demo content in a new Projection instance

---

13 Remember that these hypotheses could be completely different from the ones she probably came up with at the beginning of her study.

14 It might be argued that there is really one insight here: a lack of clarity on what to do next. The fact that there's no content may not really be an insight. It might be part of the bigger issue—that of users being unsure what to do next. That's OK. Don't get hung up on that. Whether there are one or two insights doesn't matter. What matters is that you evolve a framework around the hypotheses. What ultimately matters is that the issue is fixed.

will cause more new users to stick around longer, because it'll be much easier to figure out *what* Projection is used for.

Hypothesis 2:
We believe that including a set of instructions that teach each new user how to use the basic features will cause more new users to stick around longer, because it'll be much clearer *how* to use Projection.

Step 3. Flip each hypothesis into an invention question. Invention forms the backbone of design solutions.

Here's where you go "I know what an insight is. I also know what a hypothesis is. What, pray tell, is an invention?"

Well, an invention is the art of creating something new. In our current scenario, an invention is a design solution. Don't get hung up on the "new" part too much. If you repurpose an old invention to solve the current problem, then that will do just fine.[15] If you are good at making your insight into an actionable one, and you follow that up by creating a clear, well-defined hypothesis, you should be in a good position to start ideating on the perfect solution.

For the problem at hand, let's start your invention by asking the question—How might we introduce some content in a new Projection instance to make it easier for new users to understand *what* Projection is used for?[16]

Your design solution might take the form of a few pages of simple content that mimics what a typical user might encounter while getting started with the product. The content needs to be thought through to look realistic and reflect real-world situations.

---

15 Of course, you need to be careful that that the old invention is not the intellectual property of another company!

16 "How might we" is a concept introduced by Min Basadur (15) in the mid-'70s. It is still extremely popular and widely used in companies like Google and Facebook (16).

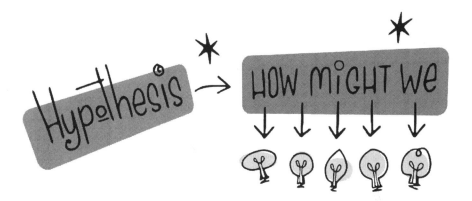

In a similar manner, your second invention could address the following question—How might we teach new users, in a clearer manner, *how* to use Projection?

Your design solution might take the form of specific help panels that teach the user how to add pages, groom their own profile, and use the WYSIWYG editor.

Step 4. Each invention in turn can be designed and tested iteratively. This not only lets you refine your designs but also helps validate the hypotheses underlying these inventions. In continuing with the above example, let's say you set up an experiment to assess your idea about onboarding panels. The experiment can be considered successful if these panels cause fewer participants to drop off during onboarding. If you discover that your panels have absolutely no effect on the drop-off rates, it could mean one of two things: your panels idea didn't work, or the underlying hypothesis—that they need onboarding help in the form of "how-to" instructions—is wrong. Either way, you'll need to go back and come up with new designs and test them. If they fail as well, then the only thing to do is rework your hypothesis. You may need to take another look at the data and redo some of the analysis. Maybe you'll even have to collect some additional data. Be prepared for that.

There you have it. Four steps from insights to design. It's a formula, and often steps leading up to invention aren't that linear—in other words, everyone comes up with ideas from the get-go—but it's a good structure to start with.

Let's recap.

Step 1.

Generate actionable insight.

Step 2.

Create hypotheses based on the insight.

Step 3.

Create inventions to translate the hypothesis into tangible design solutions.

Step 4.

Run experiments. Test the invention and examine whether the underlying hypothesis holds true and whether the solution you're created is the right one.

If your test indicates that the design solution you're created indeed works, then it means you're on the right track. It also implies that the underlying hypothesis you've created is probably true.

If your test indicates that the design solution you've created doesn't work, it could mean one of two things: either the solution is wrong or the underlying hypothesis itself is invalid. Either way, it's back to the drawing board for you, and you'll have to repeat the process outlined above till you reach the right solution. It's hard, it's rigorous, and it will ultimately yield the best solution.

Part 2
Doing effective research

This section is intended for people interested in understanding the different things that determine their effectiveness as a researcher. While this section is predominantly meant for a slightly more experienced researcher, there are a lot of things here that the rookie can appreciate as well. In other words, no matter who you are, keep reading!

6

This hair does not need splitting

The difference between marketing research and user research

"I can't believe our new vice president doesn't know the difference between user research and marketing research. We're all screwed."

—OVERHEARD IN A CONVERSATION AMONG A GROUP OF
USER RESEARCHERS

Recently, I had a conversation with a fellow researcher. Before I give you the actual conversation, here's the context.

I was trying to see if I could identify reasons why we were experiencing high product churn within the first month of purchase of one of my company's software products. Some of the research had to be conducted in the UK, as we were experiencing some significant churn there. I didn't have the bandwidth to fly to the UK, and I don't think my team had the budget to fly me there either. Also, I wanted to conduct some customer site visits, which meant I couldn't do the studies remotely. Luckily for me, one of the teams that often works with me happened to have a seasoned user researcher in the UK! I wasted no time in getting in touch with my counterpart, excited that we would be getting my study off the ground across the pond. But my elation was short-lived. Here's how the conversation went.

Me: So did you get a chance to look at the research proposal I sent you?

Him: Yes, I did. Looks like an important project.

Me: And? What do you think? Will you help me conduct the study in London?

Him: Well…umm…

Me: Is there a problem?

Him: It's just that…

Me: Go on. What is it?

Him: Well, I'm not too excited about running the study.

Me (surprised): Why not?

Him: See, things like increasing product engagement, retention, and churn aren't really my forte.

Me (even more surprised): What do you mean?

Him: See, I'm a user researcher. This project of yours—it doesn't sound like user research.

Me (now shocked): Then what does it sound like?

Him: Market research. And I don't do market research. That's not me. Sorry, man. Hey, hit me up anytime you want me to do real user research—you know, things like behavioral research, product roadmap stuff…things of that sort.

Me (hope fading away): So you're not going to take this up?

Him: Sorry, buddy. No. See if you can get a market researcher to do it for you. I'm sure we have a few of them on the ground in London.

Me: Well, thanks for your time anyway.

Him: No problem! Good luck with your research!

What just happened? Why do user researchers seem to be so hung up on whether what they're doing is user research or marketing research?[17] Is this distinction important? I have an MBA and a master's degree in human factors. I used to be a marketing manager before I got into user research. I know behavioral studies are a critical part of understanding consumers for building appropriate marketing strategies. In what way is this different from the behavioral studies done by user researchers? I looked up a lot of books and articles to find out what some of the big differences are between user research and marketing research. And during the course of my search, here's what I realized:

IT DOESN'T MATTER!

Seriously. No one cares (other than maybe user researchers). When people in a company come around asking you to do research for them, all they are looking for is data. Data that helps them make a decision. Once they get their data, they're gone. Sure, they may care about whether you did the research with the right people. And whether your research was rigorous. And whether they could extend your findings to other demographics. Things like that. One thing they don't care about (and rightly so) is what you choose to *call* the kind of research you did. You can call it user research, UX research, market research, whatchamacallit thingamajiggy research. *It doesn't matter.* Really. So for those of you who are so sensitive about calling your work user research, here's my advice to you.

Drop this book (in whatever form you're reading). Drop anything else you may be carrying—your messenger bag, laptop, smartphone, coffee

---

17 Let's put aside the distinction between user research and marketing research for a minute. Turns out, most people have trouble distinguishing between market research and marketing research as well. Is there even a difference? Yes, there is. According to Qualtrics, a company that specializes in making research tools, market research refers to research focused on gathering information about a specific market, such as consumer needs, trends, etc. (17). Marketing research, on the other hand, is the study relating to much larger marketing processes such as new product development, distribution-channel management, etc. Simply put, market research is much smaller in scope than marketing research.

mug, pet pangolin, etc. If you're indoors, step outside your building. If you're outdoors already, stay there. Take a deep breath. And repeat after me the following mantra:

"I am not going to get caught in this whole user research vs. market research thing. No one else gives a damn. And I shouldn't either. So I'm going to stop being an anal-retentive sourpuss and go back in there and do some research. End of story."

Now, please go back inside. Repeat this at least five times each day until the point hits you.

OK, now on to more serious things. Even though the distinction between marketing research and user research doesn't matter from the perspective of data collection and analysis, there are separate departments in your company that do these two kinds of research, with separate people working in them. How do you manage the overlap between marketing research and user research? What's a good division of responsibility? What's the best way to communicate and coordinate?

There are many areas where collaboration is possible between marketing and user research. A few of the areas that come to mind are segmentation, pricing, building a brand, and building a value proposition. Let's talk about two of them—segmentation and pricing.

Segmentation
This is typically in the marketing researcher's wheelhouse. Segmentation refers to dividing the market into clearly identifiable sections or segments. The segments could have common characteristics like demographics (age, location, etc.). More importantly, they should have the same wants/needs or demand characteristics. Once these segments are identified, the marketing department can then evolve specific targeting strategies for each of these segments. The product/design teams can design and build specific aspects of the product tailored to individual segments. This allows

the company to create offerings that resonate better with different customer groups, instead of following a "one size fits all" approach that they would have to go with in the absence of segmentation.[18]

The method that marketers typically follow for doing segmentation is *cluster analysis*. This technique is often used to find groups in data that share common characteristics (18). In our case, the data could be details about prospective customers. While this is a commonly used technique in marketing research, I have not seen user researchers using this technique a whole lot. That's OK. User researchers can do other things that contribute to the definition of segments.

For one, user research is really good at building psychographic models. User researchers can augment cluster analysis with a really awesome technique of their own, like contextual inquiry (a combination of behavioral observations and interviews). Combining the output from cluster analysis with data from user research will yield a segment definition that is both accurate and rich in detail.

For this kind of segmentation to happen, the user research and marketing teams need to understand the strengths that each team brings to the table. They should each put their core skills to work on the project and make sure that each team handles complementary areas of research (without an overlap). In the end, both teams should bring their data together to create a deliverable that has captured the essence of the solution both in breadth and depth. Marketers can describe the segments and come up with a plan to identify and target this segment. User research can explain why a given segment behaves the way it does, and build a predictive model of what kind of product, marketing, and pricing mix would resonate best with a given segment. Can you imagine how awesome such a collaboration would be?

---

18 I have talked to product managers and researchers in a lot of new startup companies, and I've noticed an increasingly alarming trend: they all believe their product is suitable for everyone. There is no longer any attempt to answer the question of "who is our target audience?"

Pricing

This is another area where marketing and user research can collaborate. Marketing, on its side, usually has resources and money to conduct *conjoint analysis*, a decomposition method that estimates the structure of a customer's preferences (19). In simple English, conjoint analysis is a statistical technique that tells us how people value different attributes of a product. This analysis will tell us how to price individual features that come together to make up the whole product. Marketing can give us this information. Once again, user research can give us the behavioral insights that bring pricing data to life. For instance, user research can let us know the how and why behind pricing decisions. Why do people choose to value one thing more than another? How do they evaluate the value of something? What happens to their pricing assessment when two or more features are presented together? Things of that nature.

Again, in an ideal world, the two teams putting their research skills together would produce something that is way more powerful than any one team can by itself. Not many companies realize this. When user research and marketing don't work together, who do you think loses? Marketing, with their much bigger, better-funded division that is run almost entirely by extroverts and has C-level representation? Or user research, with their tiny, modestly funded division that is populated for the most part by ambiverts and introverts, and reports into another functional area like design? What do you think?

Instead of focusing on the difference between user research and marketing research, I would recommend that you focus on how you can best leverage disparate skills and bring them together to produce more value to your company and to yourself.

Instead of focusing on the difference between user research and marketing research, I would recommend that you focus on how you can best leverage disparate skills and bring them together to produce more value to your company and to yourself.

7

Gettin' all warm and fuzzy from one end to the other

Incorporating emotions into research and design, and understanding the end-to-end product experience

"I really don't need the Apple watch. I don't want another smartphone on my wrist. Yet I wear it because it's fashionable. I also feel a sense of connection to my team as everyone around me is wearing an Apple watch."

— PRODUCT MANAGER IN A FINANCIAL TECHNOLOGY COMPANY.

"A thing of beauty is a joy forever."

— JOHN KEATS.

The first time I came face to face with the magic of packaging was with when I bought my iPod Touch[19]. It was the also the first time that I

---

19 I believe this was back in September 2007.

realized how much the right kind of packaging mattered. The texture of the box was smooth to the touch and minimalist, but still felt solid, as if held something substantial. The package was designed to not only to seduce the customer, but to build suspense. When you take the package in your hand, you are in conflict. Do you enjoy the feel of the package a little longer, or do you actually open it to reveal something even more incredible inside?

Whenever Apple releases a product, it definitely draws a crowd, no matter where in the world you look. According to the website of LineAngel, an on-demand line sitting app, one of the longest lines recorded was during the 2013 release of the iPhone 5S, at Apple's flagship store in New York, when over 1400 people stood in line to shell out some hard cash over what was then the coolest gadget they could ever purchase.

Apple has also worked hard to ensure that their devoted fan-base is not disappointed with its offerings. Great care is taken to ensure that different aspects of the product complement one another perfectly, and the overall product experience is stellar. When I say different aspects of the product, I don't just mean the main object, like the smartphone or the watch. Apple is one of the few companies in the world that has shown an obsession for perfection in everything they do. Take the Apple watch for instance. Apple takes care to ensure that customers are smitten, not just by the watch, but more importantly, even by its very packaging. Apple has made packaging an integral part of its product-purchase experience. Few other companies can even come close to providing such a complete experience. The Apple Watch package serves as a prelude to what's inside. It is a design exercise in its own right and is built to enhance the expectation of its contents.

But Apple's preoccupation with design doesn't just end with its package. Where else can you find a company that has a patented staircase in its stores? That's right. Apple (or more specifically, Steve Jobs) held a patent on the glass staircase that you find in the Apple Store (20). He also held a patent on the powerpack for its laptops, which by the way is another incredible invention. It is convenient, elegant and exudes quiet sophistication.

Apple is committed to ensuring that the customer is really, really impressed by the presentation, the aesthetics, the look and feel, the sensual joy and delight the product, the accessories, the packaging, and even the very layout of the store provide. More importantly, we understand how much of the customer's experience is emotional. And the company has nailed the emotional aspect of its products perfectly.

Apple understands that people buy stuff when they like it. That seems pretty reasonable, right? Of course, there are exceptions in cases of products that people are forced to use or purchase because their company mandates it. This happens more in the case of enterprise products. I can't tell you how many times I've talked to users who have hated the products they use but have no choice but continue to use them because that's what their team uses, or that's what "IT mandated." But by and large, people do buy and use things that they like.

Now here's a question for you: what makes you like something? For convenience, choose a product that you like—your smartphone, a bike, your favorite shoes, your favorite watch…Why do you like it?

I went around asking this question to many people. Here's what I learned:

Likeability is not a rational thing, at least not for the most part, even though people try to rationalize it. It's an emotional thing.

When they were very young, my son and daughter would give my wife and me handmade greeting cards for special occasions (at the time of writing this book, they are high-school sophomores, and they still do!). The cards usually said things like "Have a wonderful birthday! I love you," but also, interestingly, followed that up with things like "because you bought me a bike" or "because you got me my favorite cake." It seemed as if, in their own cute way, they were justifying why they loved me!

I have noticed that this quality is not uncommon, and in fact continues into adulthood. When I asked people why like their smartphones, I got answers that usually highlighted a bunch of features. The usual answers were something like "much better security" or "way more apps available for this than for any other operating system." Some went further—they spoke about ease of use, about the type of code that went into the product ("It's open source"), or even that "it has a much smaller carbon footprint than that other one." Yeah, sure. You just made a huge sacrifice and bought a really expensive cellphone it because it is good for the environment!

What most people didn't tell me was how it made them feel. There is a certain level of perceived superficiality and embarrassment in being emotionally attached to a commercially sold product (as opposed to a family heirloom), and people don't want to acknowledge it. They find it much better to tell others that any product choice they made had a "perfectly rational reason" behind it. And who can blame them? Nobody wants to acknowledge that the real reason they bought a $400 product was because they were seduced by its packaging, or because it made them look cool in front of their friends. Yet that very reason was the tipping point in their purchase decision. Emotions. Not rationality.

Emotions play an extremely important role in defining our experience. We wouldn't even have an experience worth talking about if we didn't evaluate it emotionally! Then why is it that emotions take a back seat when it comes to user research? Why does so much research revolve around assessing rational reasons for why people do things?

One reason for this is that it is easier to conduct research on a purely rational level. Emotions are messy and uncomfortable—for both the researcher and the participant. People don't usually wear their emotions on their sleeves (at least not most people!). The researcher has to do a lot more delicate work to get down to emotions. Quantitative methods like surveys are not inherently suitable to assess emotions. The best you can do on a survey is to oversimplify emotions into things like satisfaction scores or use proxies like NPS (net promoter score—where people tell you whether they'll recommend the product to their peers. I talked about this in chapter 3). But that's not the kind of research that inspires designs that captivate people. ---

————

Likeability is an emotional thing.

Another reason for this is that it is actually incredibly hard to define where exactly the emotional experience begins. In order to illustrate this, let's go on a little journey—a journey into a typical Apple fan's life. A journey in the life of twenty-seven-year-old Rick Loveless.

Rick lives in San Francisco. Originally from Minneapolis, Minnesota, Rick moved to the Bay Area of California to pursue a master's degree in computer science at UC–Berkeley. After completing his degree two years ago, Rick found a job as a software developer in one of the numerous startups mushrooming all over San Francisco. Having shaved his beard off just recently (too many guys had become beard-sprouting hipsters in SF; it wasn't cool anymore), Rick has been keeping up with all the latest trends in fashion and, more importantly, in his choice of smartphones. Rick, like many of his friends, is an Applephile. He owns a Macbook Air, an iPad, and the Apple Watch, and has managed to procure a Thunderbolt monitor each for his home and his work. (And just in time too. Apple has stopped making them!) He is now looking to upgrade his phone from an iPhone 7 to the iPhone X.

Rick's experience with the new iPhone begins a lot earlier than you'd expect. It starts with the first mention of the iPhone in social media, blogs, and websites like Macworld, CNET, and the like. He starts following the different rumors about what the next iPhone would look and feel like—lighter, more battery life, better camera, stronger screen. Of course, there's always the inevitable leak—some kid in Taiwan has managed to get his hands on the latest device and has actually broken the phone and put its innards on YouTube (a video that gets hastily removed by YouTube, but not before Rick has seen it). Yes, the rumors seem to be true. The new phone does have a better battery, and what's that? Is it possible? Does it come with facial recognition? This changes everything!

As the weeks pass, Rick gets more and more excited, although he doesn't show it. He has already saved up money for the upgrade. Then comes the official iPhone X launch, with a keynote by Apple CEO Tim Cook. Rick watched the keynote at his workplace with some of his colleagues. In reality, they "worked" from a conference room where one of his coworkers hooked up his laptop to the big TV screen so everyone in the conference room could "multitask" while watching Cook and the rest of the Apple executives unveil Apple's latest offerings. Rick is in the thick of it all, responding to the snarky comments from his coworkers—"Dude...do you even know what 3D touch is?"—and defending Apple's claim that "...you've never felt anything like it." He knows that in spite of all the cynical comments, everyone in that conference room will be upgrading to the new phone within the first week of it hitting the stores.

And Rick is a true fan. He is not going to purchase the phone online. He is going to get it at an Apple store. He has done that before. He is no stranger to camping outside the Apple store. He has been the butt of jokes from his family and friends about his Apple obsession, but he takes it all in stride. They'll never know what he is experiencing. It's not obsession; it's passion—and they'll never get it.

On the big day, when the store opens, Rick rushes in. He has been preparing for this moment. He knows a lot of the Apple Genuises working in the store and has developed a personal rapport with them over the years. That's interesting, he thinks, Matty is off for the day. But Rick doesn't have much time to ponder Matty's absence. Today is different. Today is all about getting his hands on the iPhone X. In a matter of moments, he has purchased the white iPhone X (he's always gone with white). After some quick good-byes to his pals at the store (they don't have too much time on their hands either; Rick is not the only person waiting in line!), Rick dashes off to his car in the mall parking lot.

What do you think he does as soon as he gets into the car? Rip the package open and take the phone out and examine it, right? Well, you

don't know Rick! You see, Rick is not an impulsive, crazy Apple fan. He is a committed devotee. He will not ruin the moment by ripping open the package in the car. It will have to wait till he gets home.

Once he's home, he runs to his room. He has a special place for this sort of thing. He sits down in the wingback chair by his bed. (Yes. He has a wingback chair. He is classy, our Rick.) He takes a deep breath and clears his mind. He gently removes the box containing the phone from the plastic bag bearing the Apple logo. He neatly folds the plastic bag and places it on the table next to him.

He then focuses his attention on the box itself. The fiberboard/paperboard box measures 155 mm x 90 mm x 60 mm (length x width x height). According to Apple (21), the bottom of the box is made of double-reinforced cardboard and the inset tray is high-impact polystyrene. Also, Apple claims that most of their packaging is recyclable, and the box that Rick is holding is no exception. The fiber in the box is obtained from either recycled content, bamboo, waste sugarcane, or is derived from forests that have been managed responsibly. Rick has good cause to be very happy. He is not only holding one of the best packages ever made, he is also holding a package that minimizes its impact on the environment!

The box, which is matte finished, feels elegant to the touch. The box itself is a study in design. The top of the box doesn't have reinforced walls. What makes this box unique is that it is the only box in the current iPhone lineup that features the phone face up. All the rest feature the phone face down.

Rick runs his fingers along the side of the box. He brings the box close to his nose and takes a deep sniff. Even the smell of the box is sensuous. Holding the base of the box firmly, Rick gently lifts the top. It opens with a soft "shwoop" as the snug-fitting top is gently separated from the rest of the package....Wait, did he just feel a twinge in his pants? Was he about to get an erection?

All right. Let's stop here before things get messy.

Admittedly, Rick's example is a bit extreme. Not everyone has a sexual experience opening a box that contains an electronic device. But riddle me this—how many of you have actually kept your previous iPhone boxes, long after the phones themselves have been rendered obsolete? I am not ashamed to admit that I have all my previous iPhone boxes—all of them.

This begs the question—why should a half-a-trillion-dollar company focus so much of its design muscle and resources on a friggin' box? Are they crazy? Yes, crazy about attention to detail. You see, they're onto something here. They understand that the so called end-to-end experience with the iPhone begins long before the product is even launched. The speculations on social media prior to launch, the Apple keynotes, the wait for the product to become available in stores, the atmosphere in the Apple store, the experience on Apple.com, and, finally, the packaging… All lead to one thing—an incredible experience, but still just a prelude to the product experience itself.

Suffice it to say, a lot of iPhone buyers are hooked even before they touch one. Now, if a user researcher, as a part of a customer interview, asks Rick, "Why did you buy the iPhone X?" how do you think he'll answer?

Will he go—"I really can't explain. I am emotionally and spiritually attached to the product. I love it so much I had an embarrassing experience when I first touched the package the phone came in. I'm sorry, but I need a moment here…."?

Or will he say—"It's a really cool product. There are a lot of apps on there that are only supported by IOS. The phone is an indispensable tool for me, as it keeps me in touch with my family, friends, and coworkers, and I rely on it for most of my information needs. Plus, Apple is the market leader in this area, and who better to buy it from?"

If Rick needs to be taken seriously in life (and still keep his job and his girlfriend), he'd better go with something along the lines of the second response type and never say anything like the first response. Ever. To anyone.

And if you want to be taken seriously as a researcher, you need to understand that that the real reason Rick bought the phone is outlined in the first response (which Rick will never openly admit to). Therein lies the challenge for the researcher. People don't wear their emotions or their vulnerabilities on their sleeves. Research into real emotions needs to go deep. This kind of research has to look at underlying motivations, aspirations, and goals and how they relate to behaviors. Such research is not very easy to conduct. It requires skills on the part of the researcher. It requires the ability to customize the script to the participant, as not all participants are the same, especially when it comes to emotional intelligence.

And how important are emotions when it comes to decision-making? According to Dr. Antonio Damasio (professor of neuroscience at University of Southern California and adjunct professor at the Salk Institute), it is actually not even possible to make decisions without emotions. He says in one of his books that "certain aspects of the processes of emotions and feeling are indispensable for rationality" (22).

Prof. Damasio studied people who had brain injuries with one specific feature—the injury rendered the people incapable of feeling emotions. Every other part of the brain worked normally. In one instance (23), he recounts a situation where, while talking to one of the patients who couldn't experience emotions, he asked the patient to choose what restaurant to go to that night. The patient went on for a very long time debating the pros and cons of different restaurants in a very rational manner. But he was never able to make a decision. That's because, in order to make a decision, we need to "like" one choice over another, and that can never happen without an emotional connection. It is emotion that allows a person to decide whether an outcome of a decision is good, neutral, or bad. And without it, the person does not get the "lift" that leads to effective decision-making. According to Prof. Damasio, even indifference needs an emotion to be effective! Given that, it is pretty critical for a user researcher to understand the emotional needs that dictate product-purchase decisions.

So how can a researcher assess emotions? While it is hard to just ask people about their emotional connection to something, you can get a sense of where people lie emotionally based on their reactions or responses to situations. There are few techniques for this.

In NPS surveys, for instance, a person's emotions are indirectly indicated as a response to the question "Would you recommend this product to a peer?" Participants indicate their willingness or unwillingness to recommend by choosing their option on an eleven-point scale. They are then asked to explain their choice in a textbox. In cases where the product is already launched, stats on their purchases and return purchases indicate how they felt about the product.

———

> It is emotion that allows a person to decide whether an outcome of a decision is good, neutral, or bad. And without it, the person does not get the "lift" that leads to effective decision-making.

Data scraping on social media is another avenue to assess people's collective feelings about something. Word-association tests—like sentence-completion tests, reaction cards, desirability tests, and five-second tests—are another way to assess emotional reactions. In customer interviews, the researcher can use techniques like something called "five whys"[20] to drill deep into different scenarios and uncover hidden emotions. Then, of course, there's actual observations. Nothing compares to just watching people go about their daily lives, yielding some amazing insights along the way. The point is, there are a lot of ways researchers can get to assessing people's emotional needs.

But a lot of studies today do not acknowledge that. What's worse, many researchers don't go deep enough to get to people's emotional core. As I mentioned at the beginning of this chapter, one reason is that it's much harder than just coming up with a list of findings and getting the job over with. It's harder to dig deeper, and even harder to synthesize emotional drivers and communicate this to a skeptical product team.

---

20 This is a simple, but incredibly effective technique developed by Taiichi Ohno within the Toyota Motor Corporation. Simply put, it is an iterative questioning technique where you start by asking *Why?* When you get an answer, you follow this up with another *Why?* You continue repeating this technique a total of five times until the ultimate cause reveals itself. Interesting to note that when adults do this, we call this an awesome technique. When kids do this (naturally, and with no formal training), we get annoyed!

Also, most of the time, researchers and their stakeholders are unaware that they may even need to go deep. Oftentimes, everybody is just happy with a bunch of superficial findings that masquerade as insights. I am not complaining about this. Not every research study needs to go deep. And even if it did, there are so many extraneous circumstances that dictate the extent of research that can be done during a project that the researcher is almost reduced to a helpless pawn in the game of product development.

But once in a while, you need to go deep into the emotional murkiness of your users. It's vital if you don't want to build just another product, but something that changes people's lives.

And while you're figuring out the emotional journey of your users, there is one more very important thing you need to understand: the end-to-end product experience. Almost every product company thinks the end-to-end product experience begins and ends with the product. Ask any product manager or designer. They all believe that the product experience begins when the users start their product trial. They will also tell you that the product experience ends when the user no longer interacts with the product.

This is true in case of products that are considered commodities. For instance, the end-to-end product experience with a paper plate usually commences when the user picks up the paper plate and ends when the user throws the paper plate in the recycle bin. But then you don't want to be in the business of making commodities, now do you? You want to build a product that makes a deeper impact on your users than a paper plate. And when you are in the business of building deeply impactful products, you need to understand that the end-to-end product experience does not begin and end with the product. It begins way before the user starts interacting with the product, and it ends long after the user has stopped using the product. In case of extremely personal products like mechanical watches or motorcycles, the product experience lasts an entire lifetime (just talk to a biker!) and may even extend beyond the user's death to the people who inherit those products. If that doesn't blow your mind, I don't know what will.

———

Once in a while, you need to go deep into the emotional murkiness of your users. It's vital if you don't want to build just another product, but something that changes people's lives.

8

Somewhere, someone is doing some extremely crappy work and is calling it research

Bad research, and how you can avoid doing it

"50% of all mobile phone users use our app, and love our dashboard."— After some probing, this "insight" from a researcher at a Fortune 500 company was found to be inaccurate, and then was subsequently revised to: *"50% of all the people who use our mobile phone app claim to love our dashboard"*

It is really important to accept that, as is the case of any methodological discipline, user research is also plagued by horrible things that pass for science (nonscience). In order to understand what nonscience is, we must first understand what science is. Science is a systematic study of the physical world. It is humanity's best effort in understanding and interpreting the universe around us. We gain scientific knowledge through experimentation and observation. At the heart of this effort is the scientific method.

According to the scientific method, we begin by observing some aspect of the world around us. Then we describe what we observed accurately using measures that make sense to everyone. We then proceed to question what we observed (that's where we come up with the problem statement). We hypothesize solutions or explanations. We follow this up by testing whether our explanation is true or false (we call this experimentation). If we find that our explanation is true, we accept it and move on. If we find that our explanation is false, we do two things—we refine our explanation and then we proceed to test that new explanation.

Now here's the funny thing about the scientific method. It is iterative. Everything that we've known so far—everything—is open to being challenged and even completely overthrown at any point in time. Science not only accepts this, it actually encourages it.

For instance, when I was growing up, there were nine planets in our solar system. There had been nine for decades. The last of them, Pluto, was discovered by Clyde Tombaugh in 1930 (24). When I was in school, we all went about happily with our lives, unaware that Pluto's days as a member of the select nine were numbered. Then in 2005, three astronomers, Mike Brown, Chad Trujillo, and David Rabinowitz, discovered Eris (25). It was determined to be about 27 percent more massive than Pluto (26). For a while, NASA initially described Eris as the tenth planet (27).

But then something interesting happened. We discovered that we had never really known what we meant by the term *planet*! For the first time then, we came up with a definition of the term. According to the International Astronomical Union, "A 'planet' is defined as a celestial body that (a) is in orbit around the sun, (b) has sufficient mass for its self-gravity to overcome rigid body forces so that it assumes a hydrostatic equilibrium (nearly round) shape, and (c) has cleared the neighbourhood around its orbit." By defining this term clearly, it was determined that Pluto was no longer qualified to carry the title of planet. Instead, it got relegated to *dwarf planet* (28).

———

Everything that we've known so far is open to being challenged and even completely overthrown at any point in time. Science not only accepts this, it actually encourages it.

Let's make sure we understand what happened in Pluto's case. After Pluto's discovery in 1930, based on the then understanding of what a planet was, we categorized Pluto as a planet. In 2005, after Eris was discovered, we were faced with a choice of either including Eris as a tenth planet or reexamining the very definition of the term *planet* to make sure Eris still qualified. We started rattling the cages of our understanding of planets. That is the quintessential nature of science—to never rest, and to challenge previously established frameworks of understanding. By doing this, we evolved our understanding of planets and decided to demote Pluto. Sorry, Pluto!

Of course, as is the case with any method created by humans, the scientific method has its own shortcomings. For instance, it doesn't handle serendipitous discoveries very well. And serendipitous discoveries are quite common in many branches of science, like medicine and astronomy. In fact, there are many situations where you may not even have an initial problem statement or a hypothesis. A lot of valuable discoveries have been made by people armed with just a lot of curiosity and little else. Their methodologies don't lend themselves very well to the scientific method.

In real life, a lot of science is practiced in a manner that doesn't match up to the precise methods outlined in journal articles (29). But that doesn't mean that the scientific method doesn't have merit. The scientific method is just a formal way of practicing science. It's the philosophy behind it that's crucial to science. Whether we are talking of planets or trying to interpret NPS scores, this underlying philosophy should be the same. We should constantly question ourselves, do everything it takes to gain more knowledge about a given situation, formulate hypotheses where required, test them, and be ready to pivot our understanding in the face of new evidence.

Now, there is a big difference between NASA and corporate America. For one thing, most companies do not have the luxury of waiting decades in order to understand some concepts more clearly. To be honest, most companies do not exist that long. Second, there are corporate pressures that preclude an application of science to how we understand things. Time and money are always constrained. No matter how big you are, you don't always get to hire people who appreciate scientific thinking. Even if you do, powerful executives can always override them. So you make do with what you have. But that's no excuse for some of the things that pass for science in many companies. Let's look at some of the most common scientific fallacies one can encounter, especially in the field of research, and what you can do to avoid falling prey to them.

NOT HAVING A CLEARLY DEFINED PROBLEM

Sadly, this is really very common in many situations across the board. I can't tell you how many times people have come to me with a request to conduct a particular kind of study: "I'd like you run a customer interview." "I'm looking to run a survey, and I needed your help crafting the questions." "Can you run a quick card sort for me?" The funny thing is that they have already decided on the method. And oftentimes, they don't even know why the method is required! The reason people seem to jump to conclusions and zero in on a method so quickly is that they believe they already know what the problem is. But if you really get deeper into the matter, you'll realize that people seldom know exactly what the problem is. I have already talked about it quite a bit in my chapter on thinking like a researcher (chapter 2), so I won't start on this again. But I feel passionately about it. Understand the problem clearly before trying to solve it.

OVERLY RELYING ON A FEW METRICS

MAU. DAU. NPS. Just three of the acronyms that spell religion to decision-makers. I was asked if I could find out how we could increase DAU for our product, which happened to be a software that tracks software bugs. This question is so wrong in so many ways! DAU stands for daily active users, a measure of the number of users who are actively using your product on a given day. The higher the number, the better it is for the company that makes the product, because it means their customers are using it more every day. Except in this case, the product was a bug-tracking software. If customers use the product more every day, this means they are tracking more bugs. That could mean one of two things—they are tracking bugs that they weren't tracking earlier (which is a good thing, generally speak-ing), or they are tracking more bugs because every day, their product is getting lousier and lousier (which, generally speaking, is not a good thing)! It's the same deal with other metrics. Understand what the metric really does. Understand if a higher value of the metric is good for you *and* your customer. And never get too attached to one metric. There are many ways to assess your company's success. Metrics can be intensely one-dimensional.

CONFUSING CORRELATION WITH CAUSALITY

The rise and fall of the Dow Jones Industrial Average (DJIA) has always been inexorably linked with the fortunes of baseball teams. The year

2016 was no different. The World Series in this year was won by Chicago Cubs, who wrenched victory away from the Cleveland Indians. Cubs fans around the world had waited for this event for over a hundred years— 108 to be precise. The last time the Cubs had won a World Series title was way back in 1908. Their next win would not come until the wee hours of the morning of November 3, 2016. As you'd expect, Cubs fans were elated. But they were not the only people who were overjoyed. The stock market had reason to celebrate the agonizing and intensely thrilling Cubs' victory as well. You see, before the World Series was even played, stockbrokers "knew" what a Cubs win would do to the stock market. They had seen this trend before. A win by a favored team had "sent" the stocks soaring before (in 2016, the Cubs also happened to be the favored team overall, not just by Cubs fans). After the Cubs' win in 1908, the stock market had jumped 3.4 percent over the next three months (30). After the Indians' last win in 1948, the index actually fell by 1.7 percent during the next three months. No wonder people were so excited by the Cubs' win. Clearly, there seems to be some kind of a connection between a favored team winning the World Series and the stock market's subsequent performance. It's not hard to imagine why. It makes sense to credit a team's win with the overall mood of the people, which could in turn impact the stock market. But the question is—did the Cubs' win really *cause* the stock market to rise, or was it merely a correlation? This begs the question…

What is correlation?

Consider two variables A and B. When you observe these over a period of time, you might notice that a change in A also corresponds with a change in B. The change can be an increase or decrease or a jump from one state to another, etc. This relationship between two variables is measured by correlation (31). Correlation gives us an estimate of the size and direction of the relationship. Correlation squared gives the strength of the relationship.

The key thing to correlation is that just because changes in A correspond with changes in B, you cannot infer that changes in A are actually *causing* the changes in B. Chances are, A might *correlate* with B to some extent.

Let's look at a simple example. During the month of July, you discover that people around you tend to drink more water. Your observations don't stop there. The ethnographic maven that you are, you also notice that the same people also tend to eat more ice cream. You immediately and wisely come to the conclusion that drinking more water causes people to eat more ice cream. Or is the other way around? Does eating more ice cream cause people to drink more water? This is a real head-scratcher, right? In reality, drinking more water and eating ice cream are activities that could *correlate* with one another. But one doesn't necessarily *cause* the other. The causal factor could be something that you have not considered till now—July is a summer month (at least in the state of California it is!), and the need for water and ice cream could be *caused* by an increase in temperature.

———

Just because changes in A correspond with changes in B, you cannot infer that changes in A are actually *causing* the changes in B.

The example I gave might make you go "Duh!" But in plenty of real-life examples there may not even be a relationship between two variables A and B at all, and the effect observed might be attributed to nothing more than coincidence. Yet people assume causality when none exists. Case in point—the fortunes of baseball teams and stock indices.

Getting back to my story about the Cubs and the stock market, one cannot infer that a team's performance in the World Series would somehow cause the DJIA to rise or fall. The tricky thing about correlation is that when it is observed, people are very quick to come up with explanations on what's *causing* it happen, and they infer causality even though none might exist. And user research falls prey to this more frequently than you'd imagine.

Here's another example. (I'm on a roll here—somebody, stop me please!) This one, unfortunately, is based on true events and is something of the sort you're more likely to encounter in your work life. It involves the correlation between ad spending and the number of visits to the company's website.

The primary sales channel at one of the companies I worked for was its website. The bulk of the revenue was generated through online sales. The company had a sales team, but it was small and focused mainly on large, enterprise accounts. And as it turned out, a big part of the company's revenue came from small businesses that made purchases online. Naturally, the marketing team was focused on coming up with strategies that would drive visits to the company's website.

One of the tried and tested methods to do this, of course, is running ad campaigns. The marketing team ran a campaign on some of the popular tech websites (like Wired and PCWorld). In parallel, they also put up a few billboards in strategic high-traffic areas in San Francisco, and purchased some commercial spots on a couple of popular radio channels. The combined campaign ran for about six months. Three months after the campaign ended, the marketing team wanted to assess the impact of the campaign on sales. To its delight, sales did go up by almost 10 percent. That was nothing to be sneezed at.

But should the ad campaign get all the credit? You see, while the campaign was going on, the product team was working hard to make the company's products easier to use. They had received feedback from user research that a lot of customers found the products hard to use, and this was having a negative effect on the NPS scores given by customers. So the product team worked diligently to come up with a simplified version of the company's products. Since a lot of the company's sales really happened without any help from sales, the product team contended that positive word of mouth had a lot to do with the rise in sales. To back their claim, they cited the NPS scores on the products, which had indeed gone up.

Can you see all the correlations and causal relationships at play here? There are a ton of causal factors here—starting with the campaign content and channels, to NPS scores (which reflect word-of-mouth recommendations) and aspects of simplicity and complexity of products. Are all these even causal factors, or are they actually dependent variables themselves? For instance, did customer recommendations (as indicated by a high NPS) cause a rise in sales, or did the product team's work cause the NPS to rise? What is the real causal factor here? As you can well imagine, as many as six different teams took credit for causing the sales to rise. In reality, they were all probably equally responsible (or not!).

And just to close the lid on this—what exactly happened in 2016? After the Cubs won in November, did the stock market shoot up again? Did stockbrokers around the country have cause to rejoice? Well…it's hard to tell. There was some fluctuation, but that was all. That's because something else was going on that could have had a significant effect on economic indicators. (We don't know for sure. Again, this event may or may not have been causal) This was the year of the US presidential election that saw two extremely polarizing contenders battle it out—Donald Trump and Hillary Clinton. Trump won. The election results could also have had an impact on worldwide stock numbers, clearly disrupting any effect the Cubs' win might have had. But will that deter stockbrokers from betting on the Cubs in the future? I don't think so!

NOT KNOWING HOW TO FORMULATE A HYPOTHESIS
This is so common I wrote a whole chapter about it in this very book. Chapter 3. Check it out.

TALKING TO THE WRONG PARTICIPANTS

This one. Oh boy! Why can't people understand that it is important to get the personas correct before reaching out to a whole bunch of customers? Yes, there is such a thing as convenience. I get it. You want to talk to customers who are close to you (physically and spiritually). It's the very essence of what is commonly called "guerilla user testing." But that should be reserved for very specific type of studies.

For instance, if you are looking to understand how people use work-related apps on their mobile phones, you can do a "café" study. Just walk to your neighborhood Starbucks and start shadowing people (with their permission, of course). Working on smartphone apps is a very common thing. Most people do it, and you wouldn't be remiss in studying them. But what if you're interested in something more nuanced? Something a bit different—like a study to assess how noncustomers assess your product line. And to be even more specific, let's say you are interested specifically in one user role—a DevOps manager[21]. This one's a little tougher, isn't it? For one thing, you can't just go around hoping you'll randomly bump into someone who is in DevOps. For another, the person should actually be involved in assessing software products. If not, her feedback would not be accurate.

Yet time and again, I've come across studies where researchers have reached for the most convenient demographic. Noncustomers who fit a particular user type are especially hard to find. And there is constant pressure on the researcher to wrap up the study quickly. In such cases, it is not uncommon to settle for less-than-ideal participants. I was an observer once in a study where the designer who was running the study asked an existing customer to "pretend that you're a first-time visitor to our website." Ouch! That's just plain wrong. There is no way customers should be asked to pretend to be something they are not.

So what do you do in such a case? There are two options. You wait for the right customer group to be recruited, or you try to figure out a

---

21 DevOps is a concept that unifies software development and operations.

different way to get the data you want. Maybe you should consider a different research method. If you don't find users in your immediate vicinity, then maybe you shouldn't attempt to conduct an in-person study. Maybe a remote study will give you better reach.

USING THE WRONG METHOD FOR THE WRONG QUESTION

The question should drive your research method—never the other way around. I've stated this more than once in this book because time and time again, I come across studies where this doesn't happen. What's more, I've even seen user researchers get this wrong on occasion.

The fact that the question should drive the research method is as intuitive a statement as "use the right tool for the job." This sort of thing should be self-explanatory. You use a hammer to drive a nail in. You use a drill to make a hole. You use a saw to cut, etc. Running a survey when you need an in-depth field study is as crazy as using a drill to hammer down a nail. Yet that fact escapes many otherwise intelligent people. Why is that?

> Use the right tool for the job—should be self-explanatory.

One reason for this is ignorance. If you don't know about the existence of different kinds of tools, then you'll use the one or two tools you do know about for everything. If all you have is a hammer, then everything starts to look like a nail. If the only thing you ever do to collect any kind of data is contextual inquiry, then every question starts to look like something that would need a deep, in-depth customer story for an answer. I've worked for a company that did just that. Drove me nuts.

And you can't convince such people that they should be using other tools in the tool belt. Especially if they don't know what they don't know.

Another reason for using the wrong method is what I call the *glamor factor* of research methods. Certain kinds of user research command more respect than others, especially from people outside the research field. More people prefer quantitative studies over qualitative studies just because numbers are sexier and easier to grasp. I don't mean to deny the power that numbers have. But what if all you need at the moment is a simple customer interview with five or six participants? What if you really don't need a survey with five hundred people? I've found that it's incredibly hard to convince people, especially if they are higher up the organization and I need buy-in. It's much easier to tell them I need money to run a study with five hundred customers than to tell them I need money to run a study with six customers. It just seems more intuitive to everyone. Even if that's the wrong thing to do.

So where do most mistakes happen? What methods are most misused? I have found the following methods to be most susceptible: surveys, contextual inquiries, customer interviews, and a/b tests, explained below. Other methods are subject to misuse too, but not as much as these four. And interestingly, all four are also some of the most popular methods out there. These are the glamor methods of the research world!

Survey

Surveys are great at getting quick responses from a wide swath of the target population. You can build one fairly quickly. There are tons of online tools, many of them even offering a fair degree of functionality for free. The appeal of surveys comes from the fact that on any given day you'll hear about one in some form or another. Your marketing team is running a few all the time, you read about them in the news, or you're likely to get hit with some sort of poll anytime you go online. Surveys are everywhere. And they're extremely easy to misuse.

A survey is essentially a tool used to answer the question "What." It provides a description of something. By using a survey, you obtain things like factual information, self-reported data, or opinions of people. And this information should be easy to aggregate. That's the prime purpose of a survey—to get *aggregated* information. You must make sure that the results are statistically significant.[22] You must also make sure that your sample is truly random (within the confines of the right persona of course.) These are some of the best practices for building a survey. A simple Google search will yield a lot of such best practices. So I won't go into those here. The point I'm trying to make is—if you discover that in order to get the responses you'd need, you'll have to stray way away from these best practices, maybe you shouldn't be building a survey.

Contextual inquiry

There's nothing like visiting users in their habitat. If you want to understand behavior, you should observe this behavior where it's most likely to occur. So going out to visit customers where they live or work makes complete sense. But what if the research question doesn't require a behavioral study? For instance, what if you need research to help inform the information architecture of a product? Or what if you are looking for information that would drive user segmentation? Unfortunately, certain companies would still use contextual inquiry for such research. Remember what I told you about the hammer? If the only tool you have is contextual inquiry, then everything begins to look like a behavior study.

Customer interviews

This is the easiest method of them all. What could be easier than just asking a customer a bunch of questions? And what's wrong with doing it all the time? Why conduct a detailed study to assess the usability of a feature? Why not just show the feature to the customer and ask her what she thinks about it? If you are looking to know whether a concept resonates with a customer, you don't have to mince words. Just ask directly—"Do you like this"? Hmm, what could go possibly wrong with this approach?

---

22 In case they aren't, either run the same survey with more people until you get significance, or if more people are not available, at least make sure you include a note informing people that the results are not statistically significant but are at best directional.

In case you didn't catch it, that was sarcasm, folks. If you didn't, please talk to a seasoned researcher or read a good book on research methods. There are plenty of those on Amazon. Please don't conduct research until you've done so.

A/B test

There's a certain ring to this. A/B test. You test A, and you test B. Choose the one that performs better. End of story. But there are plenty of things to be done before A and B have evolved to a stage that warrants testing. For instance, if A and B are design versions to solve a particular problem, you need to have a clear understanding of things like the problem space, who it affects, and why solving the problem is even important. There's plenty of research to be done for each of these things. And even seasoned researchers can forget to solve them, or even acknowledge that they exist.

I've seen this more when designers join the fray. Oftentimes, there's a lot of pressure on the designers to keep producing. And nobody likes it when a researcher slows things down with a "let's first understand..." way of thinking. So the researcher plays along, and before actually investigating why a solution should take a particular form, he partners with designers who, under duress, create multiple versions of a half-baked solution. And off he goes to test them. A/B test them to be precise.

MISINTERPRETING DATA

Have you heard of the story of the blind men and the elephant? If you haven't, gather around, my friends, and let me regale you.

This story originated in the Indian Subcontinent hundreds of years ago. Then, like the strong smell of a heady Indian spice, it wafted to other parts of the world. It went on to become a part the folklore of many religions, like Jainism, Buddhism, and Hinduism. Without further ado, here it is.

A group of blind men (or men in pitch darkness) happen upon an elephant. The only way they can describe the animal is by feeling it. One man touches the leg of the elephant and says, "This animal resembles

a pillar." Another feels his tail and says, "You're wrong. It's more like a rope." A third touches the belly and says, "This thing's like a huge wall. You guys are nuts." A fourth touches the elephant's ear and says, "...The heck you talkin' about? It's like a fan, you idiots." (I am paraphrasing here.)

Now, here's the thing. None of the men ventures to touch any other part of the elephant to see what the other man is talking about. They are convinced that they have grasped the entire animal and so do not see the need to explore further. They are also equally convinced that all the other men are dead wrong.

Eventually, a fight breaks out between them. Then, a woman with sight comes along (or she switches on the light) and helps the guys realize that they were all equally correct all along. It's just that none of them could see the complete picture. More importantly, none of them was willing to see another person's perspective. If a neutral third person hadn't shown up at the right time and sorted the matter out, they'd have gotten violent. They might have hurt each other, or even worse, gotten their butts kicked by the elephant—who, I'm sure, was getting pretty annoyed by a bunch random men feeling him up.

Of course, the original parable probably did not have characters who spoke so colorfully, and maybe a vicious fight did not break out between the men. But I did what every good storyteller does—embellish the story to serve a purpose. My purpose here is to illustrate something important that happens very often when a bunch of stakeholders get involved in research.

So now here's the setup. As usual, this one's based on true events. You have managed to get all your key stakeholders interested in the research you're doing for them. And you've even managed to get them to observe the user sessions with you. Now you are working with them in analyzing the data you've collected, trying to see what kind of actionable insights you can get from your study. That's when things get interesting—like the story with the elephant.

People start looking at only the part of the data that concerns them. Worse, they start making decisions on what needs to be worked on based only on their interpretation. The designer looks at the findings and locates things she'd need to fix on the UI. The product-marketing manager looks at the findings and thinks that all the evidence points to making a case for the upcoming marketing campaign. The developer sees bugs everywhere and thinks to himself, "Why can't anyone see what's most important here? It's all about the bugs. That's what our customers care most about!"

Of course, this disagreement doesn't degenerate into a physical fight. That's crazy. We live in a civilized world. We don't fight like that. Instead, like good people in technology firms, we backstab. And sabotage the study, and screw everyone else in performance evaluations. That is, unless someone with an ability to see the complete picture steps in and shows everyone what they're missing. That someone is you, the researcher. You have the unique vantage point of seeing multiple people's perspectives. And you are the one person in the room who is not obliged to dance to any particular department's tunes. That's because you represent the unseen elephant in the room—the customer.

LOOKING FOR DATA TO VALIDATE RATHER THAN ILLUMINATE

Any element of data in its purest form is just information. It makes no claim about being important or about driving decision-making. It's what you do with the data that makes all the difference. There are three aspects to making data useful. The first is collecting the right kind of data. The second is how you visualize the data. The third is how you interpret the data and draw insights from it.

I talk substantially about all three aspects throughout this book. But the one thing I haven't touched on much is the intent behind the first aspect. Now, the intent is not something that a researcher really needs to be concerned about. Anytime research is done, there should be only one intent, the ideal intent, which is to make sure the right information is collected to help make the best possible decision. But as happens ever so frequently, the decision is already made even before the data is collected! In that case, any data collected would be used to merely substantiate the decision, and not to change it or even question it.

While different kinds of research are used for validations at different stages of decision-making, I have noticed that a lot of validation research occurs toward the end of the decision-making stage in most companies. And two types of user research unfortunately fall victim to this process.

1. The usability test—This is used to assess usability issues but is also used to validate the assumptions that drove the designs. A lot of these tests do not change the design direction. They merely help address some usability issues with the UI.
2. The concept test—This is done a little bit ahead of the usability test, and concepts are not yet fully baked into prototypes. So

there is some hope that they influence the product direction a little more than the end-of-stage usability tests. But for the most part, concepts are usually pretty well fleshed out before the test begins.

So why is a lot of research done to validate? And what should data really be used for?

For one thing, data-driven decision-making is not in the DNA of many people. Most decisions made are made emotionally, not rationally (I talked about this in chapter 7). But people who make decisions at their jobs seldom acknowledge it. They shouldn't. They won't earn much respect if they do. So what little data they collect is really used to show the world that they were right all along.

For another thing, there is ignorance. A lot of people do not even think of invoking data during early-stage decision-making. Many people don't even realize that they could be making more intelligent decisions at every step throughout the product roadmap by using data. People also tend to believe that they can't test things in progress; that everything should be fully thought through and that all designs should be complete before testing. But that defeats the very purpose of testing! You need user inputs before everything is fully baked, not after all decisions have been made.

———————

Any time research is done, there should be only one intent, which is to make sure the right information is collected to help make the best possible decision.

One of the big excuses made here is that you can't show your customers half-baked designs. What will they think? As it turns out, customers understand and actually appreciate being included in the design process. I have never met a single customer who complained when I showed him work that was still in progress. There are a whole bunch of user-testing methods just for this purpose—ever heard of paper prototyping? And there are whole bunch of online tools available for early-stage testing. Just Google "user research tools" and you'll be hit with a plethora of information.

Now let me make one thing clear—it's not wrong to use data for validation. In fact, I think it's a good idea to run one last study to make sure everything that led up to the final iteration of design was, in fact, based on sound and deliberate reasoning. My gripe here is that very often, that's all that's ever done! There is hardly any research done to help in early-stage decision-making—where it matters most. Imagine what the right kind of data can do at every critical step in the decision-making process. It would make product development so much more sensible and rational—and most importantly, so much easier!

All this ultimately goes back to what you as a responsible researcher can do. It's up to you to teach your team how and when to use data. You need to show them what it means to use data for validating decisions vs. driving decisions. Part of this teaching involves demonstrating how to use data. This means you may need to go a little rogue and actually do some early-stage studies. You can then use this data to demonstrate how your team should be thinking. Your prime goal as a researcher is not to collect data, but to help people think better. Capisce?

ASSUMING THAT YOU ARE THE IDEAL USER

I was working on a budgeting product. We had just conducted a usability test on a budgeting dashboard. It was just a routine usability test, just like the ten other tests that different teams ran that month. Except this one had one critical difference. A strange twist of fate ended up making this study very visible to the entire organization. It was one of those things where a VP decided to get a little more mileage for the product. As part of his pitch to get more resources, he mentioned to his management that all aspects of his product were subject to rigorous user testing, and he used the dashboard test as an example. And for some reason, news about this test escalated further, till it reached the very top of the organization. And that's how one of the most powerful CEOs that the Bay Area had ever seen got involved. And as CEOs are wont to do, this guy dove deep into the thought process behind the feature definition. He was part of everything, including the usability test script, deciding on the kind of participants we spoke with and the findings from the study. In this case, the participants were business owners or partners. They were C-level executives of small and some midsized companies

Then he said something I thought was hilarious, except it wasn't meant as a joke. He told us that if we wanted to talk to C-level executives, we shouldn't really waste time talking to the kind of people we usually spoke with. We should use *him* as a typical example and just get his thoughts on the product. Because, as he put it, "I do budgeting too. I am a pretty good example of a typical C-level person." Except he wasn't. He is one of the richest men in the world. His net worth is more than many countries' GDP! There is nothing "typical" about him in any sense of the word. But how do you convince him that he is not? None of us had the guts to go up against him. So we humbly accepted that he's "typical" and used him as a sounding board. We had to. We felt as if our jobs depended on that.

This brings me to a very important topic—people at all levels (including investors) making product decisions because they think they are the ideal users of the product. And everyone falls prey to it, all the way from executives to the user researchers who are required to conduct objective studies on the products. It's a natural human thing to assume that when you feel something, others are likely to feel it too. And it makes sense, right? I mean, you are a normal human being (or at least you'd like to think so!). Which means you should be able to feel the way others feel, and think the way others think.

To some extent, you'd be right. In general, the environment affects all people in much the same way. A good song or a good dish usually elicits much the same emotion from people. But as you might have experienced, it's wrong to generalize across an entire population just based on how you feel. (And that's why I said "might have" experienced. I don't want to generalize. See what I did there?) You shouldn't do it even if you are a user researcher and fancy that you can get into the minds of people more easily than the average person.

Does that mean you should not rely on your gut at all? No. Far from it. Rely on your gut—but only to come up with hypotheses, or to make educated predictions about what might happen. But don't draw conclusions based on them. At all times, use real users for this—people who will be part of the real audience of the product. Never compromise on this, even if the product you're evaluating is a tool for user researchers! You will be wise to evaluate with other user researchers; don't use yourself as a test participant for your studies—ever.

NOT RECOGNIZING YOUR BIASES

In this chapter, I have just scratched the surface of what you should be aware of as a user researcher. There are plenty of topics that I have deliberately not covered, or covered in great detail—for instance, biases and the mischievous role they play in a researcher's life. Covering biases is such a big deal that I could write a whole book on it. But thankfully, I don't have to. There are many good books already written on this topic.

But I will say this about biases. They tend to creep up on you when you're not looking. You could convince yourself that you're the most unbiased human on this planet, but you'd probably be wrong! And here's what you need to know about biases. They are nature's way of helping you deal with the world around you. And they are not inherently all wrong. For instance, assuming that food from a certain part of the world would be spicy would actually make you a bit more careful about putting a large chunk of it in your mouth (that's a stereotyping bias, by the way). That's OK. You are protecting your tongue from getting scalded by spice. But using a racial stereotype to reject a candidate during a job interview? Now, that's all kinds of wrong!

The trick about biases is to acknowledge that you are as susceptible to them as the next person. Once you acknowledge this, then you can understand how to counter it. And you can help others learn how to mitigate its effects too. That's how you'll earn the respect of your peers—by being a conscious researcher who is capable of recognizing your own bias and the damage it can do to your ability to make good decisions.

9

Print that report in Comic Sans! And other fun ideas to make your product team cry

Examining your deliverables

"I have to help my team's researcher make a report that pops out visually. Researchers who make visually stunning reports get a chance to present at our staff meeting, and have a shot at getting more people to look at their recommendations."

—Visual designer at a major social-media company

"Don't make it look like you're telling people what to do. Use a tone where you seem like you're merely suggesting improvements. The product manager will make the final decision anyway. Plus, we don't want to offend our designers."

—Design manager to me

Let's talk about recommendations. Here is an excerpt from a user-research report:

Issue: *"Participants had trouble locating the save button. That was because some pages implicitly performed the save function and there was no save button on the page, and in the case of other pages, the participants had to explicitly click the save button."* This issue was marked with a severity of 3 on a scale of 1 to 5. A score of 3 is midrange. Not too severe, but important enough to be fixed. The report also noted that out of the eight people who participated in the test, five of them had a problem hitting the save button.

Recommendation: *"The save model should be consistent through all pages of the workflow. Make sure that the save button is included prominently at the top and bottom of every page."*

Here's another excerpt from a different report:

Issue: *"Participants could not read the text in the callouts used for onboarding because the text was too small."*

Recommendation: *"It is recommended that the font size of the text in the callouts be increased."*[23]

THE "DUH" RECOMMENDATIONS

A few things are immediately evident from both the recommendations given above. First off, there is the obvious nature of the recommendation (hence the name "duh" recommendations–they make you go "duh" when you read them!). If the font size is too small, increase it. If a button is not visible, make it bigger and more prominent. You'd be surprised how many user-research reports make these "duh" recommendations. Why would you even need to run a user test to ascertain these so-called "issues"? Do you need a bunch of people to tell you that the font size is

---

23 Notice the passive voice and tone of the recommendation. Can the writer be more vanilla?

too small? Can't you see that for yourself (or in this case, can't you *not* see it for yourself)? You really don't need validation from users to fix every small thing.

The problem with making such recommendations is that the researcher who wrote this not only devalues himself as a researcher, he kind of devalues his whole profession. Since he'll be saving this report for posterity, his half-assed recommendations will continue to survive long after he has left the company. Nice going, genius!

Now here's something he could have done that would have made him look a lot smarter—in the case of the save-button issue, he could have found out why customers would need to save their work so many times. From the usability issue observed, it seems there are multiple pages where people need to save their work. Why are so many pages required? What kind of information are users saving? Is there any way to avoid the requirement to enter so much information? Gross inconsistencies like having auto-save on a few pages but an explicit manual save on others could indicate that different teams were responsible for the two experiences. Why is development split that way? Maybe the real reason for the problem with the save functionality is the way the company's internal teams are organized. Maybe the problem is really inside the company, and the customers are just hapless victims (as is usually the case).

In the case of the callouts, the researcher's work would have been more valuable had she questioned the need for the images with callouts. Why is there so much text in the callouts in the first place? Can the information be delivered in a more elegant way without using callouts? She could have worked with a visual designer to figure out what exactly is going on and why. Then she could have come back with some proposals for design changes that didn't require the use of callouts. She could have explored different options before coming up with a recommendation.

And that's good advice for any researcher: never make your stakeholders do the work that you can do. Try to do as much of the work as you can. That way people will see that you're committed to finding the right solution, and you can have more involvement in the project's success.

THE "MEH" RECOMMENDATIONS

Then there's what I'd like to call the "meh" recommendation. This is more interesting than the "duh" recommendations. Take a look at this example from a different study.

> **Issue:** *"Participants felt that the amount of details collected during sign up was too much. The sign-up form was too long. In addition, participants did not know why information like industry type, and the number of people the participant works with on a daily basis is even relevant to the process of signing up."*
>
> **Recommendation:** *"Reduce the size of the sign-up form. Determine the necessity of the fields mentioned. If they are deemed unnecessary, remove them from the form."*

Sign-up forms are always tricky. Most companies like to collect information from prospective customers. This is a good thing. This gives the company a chance to understand their future customers better. They may even use this information to tailor the product to the customer's needs, which is good for both the customer and the company. But from company to company, there are vast differences in the amount of information that they collect from prospective customers. Some companies wisely collect very little information up front, just the basics—maybe the prospect's contact information and couple of other things. Others decide they need to collect a lot more information in order to build something that is meaningful to the prospect.

In the case of the situation in the example, there was a necessity to collect information about the prospect's industry type. The product functionality and performance would change significantly depending on the industry using it.

———

Never make the stakeholders do the work that you can do.

Also, since the product in question was a collaboration tool, it was important for the company to get information about how many people the prospect worked with on a daily basis. The company knew these questions were important. But on the sign-up form, these questions were asked abruptly, and with no accompanying explanation. Further, this information was collected via text boxes that were marked as required. In general, people don't like being forced to type out stuff in text boxes, much less when they are just signing up for a product trial. So they complained.

What should the researcher have done in this case? Instead of just stating that the necessity of these fields should be "determined," the researcher should have worked with his team to figure out the underlying reasons behind the lengthy form, and the two specific questions that the participants had trouble with. If the team feels that they absolutely need prospective customers to fill in this information, then the researcher should explore different ways of collecting this same information. Maybe it can be collected later during the process. Maybe some of the information like industry type need not even be collected up front. If you just know the prospect's company name, you can look up the industry type on Google. There are simple online tools available to automate such queries, so you don't have to do the physical search for each prospect yourself.

Also, the information regarding the number of people the prospects works with could be collected in the form of a question with drop-down options. Prospects would be required to just click the right option available. This is easier than typing things in a textbox.

When a researcher doesn't consider all this, but just gives a recommendation like the one in the example above, he is really demonstrating his lack of enthusiasm in making the recommendation (hence the name "meh" recommendation!).

Remember that every single recommendation is an opportunity for you to demonstrate your depth in domain knowledge, your interest in the project and your enthusiasm in making a difference. Such "Duh" and "Meh" recommendations will not do much to change the product, and may even harm your career in the long run.

You cannot make meaningful recommendations if you don't have the context around the problem space. You can get context by working closely with different stakeholders and understanding why things are the way they are. Without proper context, all you'll be able to do is come up with are "Duh" and "Meh" recommendations at best. That's one of the main reasons why research fails—making shallow recommendations without fully immersing yourself in the problem space. After making these recommendations, you should also know how to package your findings. That's where your deliverables come in.

THE MASSIVE TOME

I've noticed that on many occasions, the researcher ends up delivering something that is completely not appropriate to the situation at hand. The deliverable is the tangible output of the researcher's work. After all the data collection, analysis, findings, and insights, if the researcher doesn't have a proper deliverable to show for all the work she did, she might as well have not done anything at all.

The shape and form of a research deliverable has changed over the years. To see what some of these were and why they were probably not the best things a researcher could have come up with, let's take a walk down memory lane and start around the year 2000, when web usability was just beginning to become a discipline of its own. Web applications were few and far between. There was no such thing as cloud computing. This was still the age of server applications. People tended to work in cubicles. They couldn't take their work home, because they worked on desktop computers. Man, I miss that excuse! Now, I can never leave my work behind. Frikkin' thin, lightweight laptops with broadband Internet have ruined my life!

Anyway…user research was called something archaic like "human factors engineering" or "usability engineering." And that was quite accurate too. Researchers focused quite a bit on running usability tests for the most part. There was not much research done to drive other parts of the product roadmap. There was limited engagement between the researcher and the other members of the team. Researchers were not expected to do much else. And the deliverables? Well, let's see now.

To start with, there was the usability report. It contained everything—from an executive summary to a table of contents. There was a detailed description of the methodology and recruiting procedure. There were also the obligatory pictures of the usability lab and its two-way mirror, with a participant staring at the monitor and the researcher and a tiny group of observers on the "dark side." Good reports also had a couple of paragraphs detailing things like the facial expressions of the participants while they were doing the tasks. And then there were metrics—time on task, error rates, and satisfaction scores. At the end of the report, there were appendices for the academically inclined. There were also lots of recommendations in the report. The only thing the report was missing was an ability to keep its reader awake.

I have yet to meet a person who has read a usability report cover to cover (other than the researcher who wrote it). Anyone who says he has read a complete research report authored by someone else is either lying or has serious mental issues. In either case, stay the heck away from such people! Interestingly, there are still companies that require this kind of format for the report of a usability study. And even more interestingly, there are still researchers who happily produce this kind of deliverable, and even justify its existence, in this day and age.

What's the thinking behind writing a whole tome every time a research project is completed? And why are researchers the only people in the company who do this? Have you ever seen a developer write a report? How about a product manager? Or a product-marketing manager? They all need to document stuff too. The only other people I see composing such voluminous reports are the good folks in finance who write their company's annual reports. They need to do this because the law requires them to, so they are forgiven. There is no law that requires a user researcher to write books after each project is done. Yet researchers do it. Why?

I asked them.

They told me it's for posterity. What if someone wants to refer back to the study six months later? Yes, that does happen. It happens infrequently, but it does happen. But that still didn't justify a whole book. So I dug deeper. And here's what I came up with. It has a lot to do with two things: the nature of a researcher, and the way they engage with other teams.

Researchers are meticulous. They are detailed. And they like to share all the information they have collected and talk in detail about it. Now, if they actually try talking about all this, people lose interest and walk away. So when they are asked to write about it, they don't know when to stop. They just keep going, until they have put pretty much every single word they can think of into their reports. I can say this. I am a researcher. Many years ago, I wrote big honkin' reports too.

Then there's the engagement model. Researchers are rarely an integral part of a team. Even if they officially report to a team's manager, they still aren't fully along the journey. They miss out on the planning meetings. Sometimes they aren't even invited to such meetings, as stake-holders believe they are not needed. More often than not, the researchers don't get to sit next to key decision-makers. In such cases, the researchers miss out on crucial "hallway conversations." A lot of decisions are in reality made outside conference rooms, and if the researchers are not an integral part of the team, they miss the chance to affect such conversations and the resulting decisions.

So the only way a researcher has to make a convincing point is to put every damn thought into her report. She tries to come up with a case that's sufficiently compelling to make the changes she believes the customers would appreciate. If this compelling case needs to take the form of a volu-minous report, then so be it. Trust me, no researcher really wants to write these big reports. Researchers hate writing them as much as people hate reading them. A voluminous report is kind of the researcher's desperate attempt at demonstrating how much work and thought went into getting customer feedback to answer the research question.

Unfortunately, these large reports actually confound the very pur-pose for which they are written. When researchers present someone with such a report, they are immediately seen as people who "don't get it"— as in "they don't get the fact that I have a life, and I need information in small, easy-to-digest packets." If the researcher keeps at it, she is soon alienated and isolated, exacerbating the very problem she was trying to solve.

THE POWERPOINT SLIDE DECK

The next famous deliverable was the PowerPoint slide deck. This con-tained slide after slide of screenshots. There were elaborate callouts, some of them even color coded to indicate the severity of the issue observed. Clever, daring researchers sometimes even got away with calling this their "test report." This form of a report still exists today. And I can't say it's too terrible. It gets the job done and is a good way to preserve the state of designs for posterity. But it is still a report, just like the big usability report I talked about above. It doesn't fix anything by itself; it just tells people what to fix.

Of course, "report" is a general-purpose word to detail the findings from any kind of study, not just usability tests. There are different kinds of reports for different kinds of studies, ranging from those built for competitive evaluation to those built to detail Information architecture of a product. Some are much more modern too. I don't recall a whole lot of tree testing[24] done back in the day, for instance.

OTHER DELIVERABLE FORMATS

Then there are deliverables like personas, storyboards, and journey maps. These are meant to do things like stimulate ideas, guide thinking, and set a direction for the product-development process. They are good because they serve a very clear purpose, and they take the recipients of the report to new places in their brains. Finally, there are deliverables like wireframes, prototypes (both static and interactive), concepts, and interaction models. These are representations of what could be the final product. The user researcher usually collaborates with designers, product managers, and developers in building such deliverables. They are even more advanced in terms of getting close to the end goal. But they are still steps away from being considered the best deliverable.

WHAT IS THE BEST DELIVERABLE?

What is the holy grail of all deliverables? *Quite simply, the best deliverable is the product itself.* In fact, I would consider the product the only deliverable worth striving for. If your work doesn't show in the final product, you are wasting your time and your employer's money. I, too, am guilty of running countless studies that haven't affected the final product. This book is part atonement for that fact.

———

The best deliverable is the product itself.

---

24 Tree testing is a technique used to evaluate a hierarchy of categories. It is commonly used to assess if people can find things on a website.

OK. The product is the only deliverable that matters. What about the rest of the stuff I have been talking about, all the reports, posters, journey maps, and so on? How should you evaluate the usefulness of these deliverables? Should you survey all researchers and ascertain which deliverable their stakeholders value the most? Can you rank them in order of importance? Can you use this final list as a guide on what deliverable you need to produce after a test?

For the love of all things holy, please don't do that! It's this kind of thinking that has been the bane of user research all along: this aspect of finding what different people think is effective and then catering to that. Researchers always try to please everyone all the time—and screw themselves up in the process. When it comes to deliverables, don't ask anyone. Drink your own champagne (or eat your own dog food if you're into that sort of thing). If you're a researcher, you should usability test your own deliverables and find what works best for your audience.

But in the meantime, here's a rule of thumb to ascertain what deliverable will be useful.

The most useful deliverables:

- …answer the research question as accurately as possible. Of course, this also implies that the research question is carefully constructed. Otherwise, the deliverable is sure to miss the mark. You will need a good bit of initial preparation in defining the question and ascertaining the kind of deliverable that will hit the mark. Measure twice, cut once.
- …affect crucial aspects of a shippable product. What aspect of the product is the deliverable addressing? Is it just UI issues? Does it address product functionality? What about product performance? The more aspects that the deliverable addresses, the more useful will it be for the entire team.
- …provide avenues to possible actions that can fix the problem. A good deliverable will make it easy to see different actions that the team can take to fix the problem.

- …are timely. If there is no time to act on your report, then preparing it has been wasted effort.
- …are simple easy to understand—they don't use technical jargon. You can use things like confidence intervals and ANOVA. But keep that part hidden. Show the stakeholders only what's relevant to them.

Notice that the above rules of thumb left out one thing—the format of the deliverable. Should it be a concise and crisp report? Should it be a presentation? What form should the deliverable take?

Actually, the effectiveness of the deliverable is format agnostic. What is key with the deliverable is whether or not the information is communicated effectively. Remember that the main purpose of the deliverable is communication of information. You need to find a way to communicate this information effectively. The format in which you communicate this information is really not important.

Think about it this way. The path in front of you and your stakeholders is dark, and nobody is clear on where to go next. You, the researcher, have the opportunity to show the way. You need to take leadership and lead people to the promised land through the darkness. It doesn't matter what deliverables you use to show the way. What matters is that you show the way.

A product-marketing manager once approached me with a question: "Do we need to provide our customers with a product page that starts by letting them decide whether they need to see the cloud version of our products or the server version of our products?" I did my research to answer this question. I didn't have time to put the findings down on paper, as I was busy with a dozen other things. Luckily for me, the day after I finished my analysis, I bumped into the PMM in the hallway. She asked, "Are you done with your analysis? What should we do?" I replied, "My research has shown that most of our customers [in the demographic we were considering] have already made the decision well before they come to the website. So there's no need for that page."

She went, "Oh cool. I'll scrap plans for that page then. You can send me a write-up on your findings later. Thank you very much!"

Mission accomplished.

The deliverable was the one sentence I gave her verbally. It got the job done. Of course, when I found some time later, I put all my findings on a web page and shared it with her. But I don't think she even read it. She had the answer she was looking for.

Other formats that have been very effective are things like emails, workshops (especially if you can get all key stakeholders to participate), and discussions. One particular way to communicate the information that works really well for me is to sit with the designers and product managers when they are actually building the product. They ask me right there what they should be doing, and I simply tell them based on what I've learned from research.

"B...b...but," you say, "aren't researchers meant to produce deliverables? How will they show their work otherwise? And what about posterity?" Oh, the posterity!

My suggestion that even a conversation can be a deliverable will horrify you only if you see the researcher's job as producing deliverables. If you see a researcher as a person who actively influences product development in all its aspects, then the deliverable is actually a "nice to have" byproduct of research. The researcher's value to the company is much more than just being a "deliverable producer." The researcher's job is to make everyone else smarter by providing them with accurate and timely information. No one cares what the format of the information is.

As for "showing your work"…if you are working in a company where your manager assesses your effectiveness by the quality of deliverables you are expected to produce, and if by "quality" the manager means things like format, imagery, and efficacy of written language, then that's really sad. That means your manager doesn't really understand research. There are many such managers out there. If you are a researcher, I hope you are not working for a manager like that.

Now, what about posterity? Yeah, by all means, document stuff for posterity. It's a necessary evil. You have to do it. But never let anyone tell you it's the most important thing you should be doing. In your list of priorities, this needs to be fairly low. Your first priority is to do awesome work. If you don't do that, why bother documenting it for posterity?

All right. Here's what we've learned so far.

When we think of providing deliverables, we need to think of two things.

1. The format of our deliverables
2. The quality of the stuff we put in our deliverables

The best form that a deliverable can take is that of the product itself. Everything else we create (our reports, our workshops, our slide decks) is in service of the product, and is only useful as long as it has the ability to influence the product.

Hand-in-hand with the format of the deliverable is the quality of the deliverable. If the deliverable doesn't get to the root of the problem, the solutions that it ends up providing are superficial and shallow. A good deliverable demonstrates the painstaking hard-work, curiosity, intelligence, and interest of the researcher. It is a great opportunity for the researcher to showcase her talent and rigor. Researchers get few opportunities to succeed. The deliverable they produce is one of them.

Part 3
Doing successful research

This section is good for product managers, designers, anyone managing research teams, and of course researchers. If you are in any way connected with making user research as a functional discipline succeed in your organization, this section is for you.

10

The conundrum of chronic complexity

Making a product complex and simple at the same time

"I think it's time we focused on making our product simpler."

—HEAD OF DESIGN, REGARDING A SOFTWARE PRODUCT THAT HAS BEEN IN THE MARKET FOR OVER TEN YEARS

Does research drive features, or do features drive research? What does the universe desire? When are you putting the cart before the horse? As it turns out, the answer is not crystal clear. Because both options are OK, and both options have their own issues.

If research drives features all the time, you have what I call *customer driven innovation*. There is a problem with this approach. As Henry Ford is purported to have put it, "If I had asked people what they wanted, they would have said faster horses." It appears that Ford never really said that (32), but that's not the point. The point is sometimes really creative ideas come forth from sheer genius and inspiration (and I harped on it quite a bit in chapter 1). And not all these ideas originate from talking to customers or doing user research. Sometimes people have to rely on their own gut feel and inspiration. They have to take the proverbial plunge, with

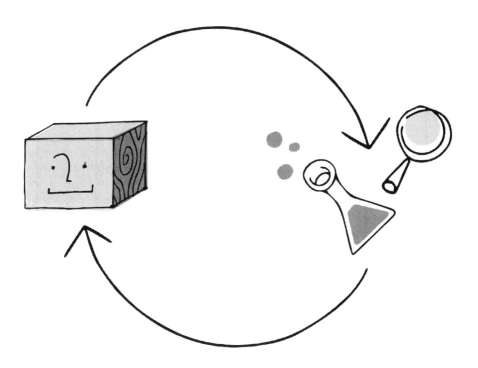

complete faith in themselves and their creations. A great number of inventions were successful because of this approach. Take the Rubik's Cube for instance. A puzzle that was originally invented as a classroom aid to demonstrate spatial relationships, it has now found its way to practically every corner of the globe and remains one of the most popular toys in the world (33). It has even experienced a return to favor in the twenty-first century. Also, let's not forget serendipity. From Corn Flakes to Velcro to Post-It Notes, a lot of inventions just happened by serendipity (34).

So yes, success *is* possible without research. And in some cases, too much early-stage research may even impede the early momentum required in product development and ideation. But this is more the exception than the rule. Unfortunately, a lot of companies now believe that creativity without the benefit of research is the norm. Over and over, I've seen product managers and designers quote the quotation misattributed to Henry Ford (smugly, I might add), reiterating that research doesn't really drive creative inventions.

That, my friend, is a load of horse manure. More often than not, customers drive and refine innovation. Even if the initial idea was not the result of a customer research study, but was someone's sheer stroke of genius, customer input almost always has to be factored in during later stages of the product-development process. This input need not have been solicited by sending professional researchers out into the field every time, but believe me when I say that, in the vast majority of cases, an invention cannot be successful if customers did not participate in giving feedback about it at some stage during the development process.

With any invention, I'd argue that some research does happen in one form or another in order to perfect that invention. Even if research isn't formally done, there's always a channel for obtaining customer feedback. The Wright brothers invented a flying machine. But if other people had been unable to use it (both as pilot and as passenger), the airplane might never have seen the light of day. A great chef can come up with what she thinks is a mind-blowing recipe. But if common customers don't like the taste of it, and other less-accomplished chefs are not able to replicate the recipe, it would die a tragic death. And where do you think your favorite actor would be if moviegoers (i.e., customers and even critics) didn't think his performance was worth watching?

———

Success is possible without research. And in some cases, too much early-stage research may even impede the early momentum required in product development and ideation. But this is more the exception than the rule.

Now, let's look at a situation when features drive research all the time. Let's call this *stakeholder driven innovation* (or *investor driven innovation* if it's a venture capital funded company) Interestingly, there are way more instances in any company when this happens. When a new product is being conceived, the team tasked with coming up with the initial concept is usually small. This makes sense from an economic standpoint. The company has not yet started generating good revenue from the product. So they want to keep overheads (material and resources, including human resources) low. For the first few months (or even a few years), there is enough work to be done on the product just to get it to an acceptable state. When the product is completed enough to demonstrate the value it brings to its users, it is launched. So far so good. As the product starts becoming successful and generating more revenue, companies decide to invest more in that product. By invest, I mean throwing more people into the mix, building more features, coming up with more ways to use the product, solving more problems, and solving more complex problems. Before long, the size of the team that is actively working on building the product grows. There is now a VP of product development in charge of all this. As it is always the case when you have a huge team, you gotta keep doing something with all those people.

You have to make your team members earn their keep—in Silicon Valley lingo, you have to "in the spirit of continuous improvement, augment the feature set in order to provide a more seamless and synergistic experience so that the product evolves to become the backbone of the customer's ecosystem." (I made this sentence up, but it sounds *so* Silicon Valley!)

And so it begins—a crazy product-development roller-coaster ride that is very common in the tech industry. I call it the *conundrum of chronic complexity*. And here's the kicker: research gets to go on this ride! Well, researchers are actually sitting the back seat here, not really driving anything. But at least they are going all the way! Yay! For your reading pleasure, let's go on this ride with them. Here's how it starts.

Consider a product that's making a good bit of money. Also, let's assume that this product is enjoying the attention of a significant part of the company, and that there's a huge team of people behind it.

During each release cycle, the product team decides to keep adding new features till the product reaches a bursting point. They do this for two reasons.

- Reason #1: Investors in the company need to see constant "improvement" to the product features. Otherwise, they get worried that their money is going nowhere.
- Reason #2: The product managers need to earn their keep. The best way to do this is by coming up with more and more features.

A lot of interesting things happen when a product becomes overly feature heavy. For starters, it becomes so complex that very few people outside the company can even figure out what to do with it. And the process a customer has to go through to be able to use it successfully becomes extremely tedious. The customer can no longer just buy it and start using it. No siree Bob! There are multiple complex steps involved here. And boy, are there some ravishing research opportunities embedded in each step! If you can't see them yet, don't worry. I'll spell it out for you. That's why I'm here.

There are six major areas of research here: training, documentation, product trial, onboarding, certification, and the quest for simplicity.

Training

Let's talk about training first. Now that your company has made the product as complex as possible, you can offer training to customers on using different parts of it. You have to. There's no way people can figure out how to use it on their own. Most large enterprises now have a training wing that falls under the highly aspirational name of *university*.[25] The training wing needs to know what areas they can provide training in. This calls for some exploratory research. Both qualitative and quantitative methods apply here. Go talk to customers. Run surveys. Find out what areas of the product are complex, and where the customers will get the most benefits. Once this is done, you'll have to help your company figure out the format of the training and where they can provide access points to the training. For instance, can some forms of training be administered within the product, while others go through a separate training tab on the company's website?

Documentation

Documentation is vital because most customers are too busy to spend time taking formal training in the product. They have other things to do, like their day jobs for instance. Plus, they probably don't want to spend

---

25 The "university" concept is a big money earner for enterprise companies. It makes so much money, in fact, that the company actually benefits from keeping the product very complex. That way, the customers will have to get formally trained in using it. There is a whole ecosystem of smaller companies (outside the big enterprise) that make money solely training people in using the enterprise company's products. A lot of these companies are actually started by people who were engineers or product managers in the enterprise company at some point in their careers! This whole ecosystem will cease to exist if the product becomes simple. Most researchers don't get this and naively recommend that the company should simplify the product. Yeah, good luck with that!

obscene amounts of money to get formally trained in using products that are supposed to be self-taught for the most part anyway. So the only way they can learn the product and troubleshoot when things go wrong is by reading up on documentation. And here again, research plays a key role in helping the company understand the user behaviors related to documentation. When do they use documentation? How do they look for it? What do they do with the documentation? Do they just use it for themselves, or do they use it as part of their own internal training program? The list goes on. All these questions are right up the researcher's alley.

Product trial

Another crucial area. Companies struggle with this one all the time. No one knows exactly how to administer product trial. For one thing, how long should the trial last? Companies want to make sure they give enough time to prospective customers to try the product out. But they don't want to wait too long; they want to monetize this opportunity as quickly as they can. And that's where they screw up. I have been in enterprise software companies where complex software like that used for project management was offered on trial for just two weeks. Two weeks! That's not even enough time to set the damn thing up, let alone try it out with real data! Then there's all the support that needs to be given to customers to help them set up the product properly. Again, instead of helping customers with everything they've got, companies get too greedy and try to minimize the support they're giving customers. "No point spending money on a prospect even before they pay us," goes the logic. But if you don't make a good first impression, how on earth do you expect your customer to like you and eventually buy your product? Oh, the humanity! Research needs to step in here and help people make some sane decisions!

Onboarding

Onboarding is the unhappy twin of product trial, and the fourth major area for research opportunities. Product trial and onboarding go hand in hand, and because they do, they are both equally messed up. Onboarding is one more area where companies need professional help. The reason companies execute onboarding so badly is because they are so inwardly facing. They can't imagine that customers would have any kind of trouble learning how to use the product themselves. "We could use it the first time around, couldn't we? Then why would the customer have any problems?" The answer is "Because you built the product, numbnuts, and the customers didn't! Of course, *you* don't need any onboarding!" So, once again, research is required here as well. A researcher needs to help the onboarding team understand how to onboard customers once they've bought the product. That ought to keep the researcher busy for a good six months at least.

Certification

Certification is, in many ways, the culmination of the product journey for a customer. Every typical journey begins with product trial, then moves on to onboarding, to product usage, to the development of expertise, and then finally ends in the crowning glory of certification. A certified user is like a sensei in martial-arts lingo. She is now ready to impart training and implement the product herself. It is a great moment in the life of a loyal customer. It means that the company that manufactures the tool she so looks up to has finally acknowledged her loyalty and expertise.

Of course, you do realize that most of this is complete baloney. In a vast majority of cases, the product really does not need to be so damn difficult that people need certifications to claim expertise in it. It is just part of the vicious cycle of product development. You put enough people and time in constantly iterating on a product and adding new features, and soon enough you end up making the product so complex that customers need to spend the better part of their careers mastering it, not to mention paying a boatload of money to the company's university.

And does research play a part in this? You bet your bottom dollar it does! Companies need help figuring out the "study plan" to administer. How do they package this training and certification? What is the best way to deliver the instruction? How much of this stuff can be taught online, vs. in person? And what forms can the online training take? Can it be via documents and prerecorded videos, or should it be instructor-led online courses? How much should they charge for this training? And when is someone ready to be certified? Even questions as mundane as "What should the certificate look like?" are thrown in the researcher's lap. That's some serious job security for the researcher right there!

The quest for simplicity

Finally, we arrive at the holy grail, the pinnacle of our conundrum—the quest for simplicity. The most sought-after product feature of all is not even a feature. It's a quality. People need the product to be simple. And given what we've been seeing about feature overload, that's the one thing that is incredibly hard to do. A "simple software product" is almost an oxymoron. It's also the most ludicrous of all product requirements.

Companies spend every cent they have in making their product as complex as possible. During the first few years, that's OK, even desirable, and customers appreciate it. But constantly adding meaningless feature after meaningless feature year after year finally starts taking its toll. Customers start complaining. But the company still doesn't care.

Like an ancient Roman general asking for more food and wine at an orgy, product managers ask for more features relentlessly. Finally, the customers have only one recourse—they stop buying the product and move to simpler competitors. At this point, any company with half an ounce of sense should stop adding more features and even start cutting down on them. But no. That seldom happens. Instead, the company continues to add features. But get this—they ask the user researcher to figure out how to make the product simple at the same time. This is quite possibly the stupidest request any researcher will ever encounter in his or her career. Advocating for simplicity while constantly adding features is like advocating for celibacy while having sex. Having a user researcher run around to find "causes of simplicity" will not solve the problem. You need to stop screwing up your product first.

The most sought-after product feature of all is not even a feature. It's a quality—simplicity.

Anyway, the poor researcher has a lot to figure out with this one. First off, what does simplicity even mean? It is a deep concept. No two people understand it the same way. And no two people will ever agree on what really needs to be done to make a product simple—especially if the solution doesn't include reducing the feature set. The kind of findings and insights the researcher comes back with is anybody's guess. Since the team will not accept any real solution that recommends a reduction of the feature set, anything the research does is like putting lipstick on a pig. And since the problem will never be solved, that's more job security for the researcher!

So there you have it. The conundrum of chronic complexity.

All right. So what have we learned so far? That products tend to become extremely bloated with features that render them almost inoperable without a ton of help from the people who made the products. We also learned that because of this, research actually has a lot of opportunities in helping the company come up with "solutions" to help customers make sense of these products.

But that's not all. There is something more important at play here. The kind of research I've been describing is actually something companies frequently do to aid in creating solutions to the complexity problem. This kind of research is entirely *reactive*. It is post-hoc research that is more like a Band-Aid than a vaccine. In reality, a lot of the research mentioned above is not required, or should not be why a researcher is hired in the first place. For instance, determining the best method of delivering technical education about how to use the product—do you even need research for this? I mean, isn't there enough literature available in the field of education to throw light on such questions?

But the problem is, most teams don't know what else they should do. For every company that wants to grow, the choice of adding more features to the product seems obvious. The other benefit of adding more features is that in order to build and manage them, the product and development teams need to grow too, leading to more opportunities for promotions.[26]

Now, how can we be smart about this whole process? Being smart involves a complete change in the very philosophy of product development as it is practiced in most enterprises. What I'm proposing will still keep the product team busy, but in a smarter way.

To look at what this "smarter way" is, we need to go back to the early days of the product, back when it was still an idea in someone's mind. You take this idea and you build a minimal viable product, fondly called MVP.[27] Eric Ries, author of *The Lean Startup* (35), came up with the concept and definition of the minimum viable product (36). I'm not going to reinvent this wheel and talk about how to build one. Eric explains all that very well in his book. What I am going to talk about here is what to do so you don't bloat your product with unnecessary features.

FOUR STEPS TO KEEP YOUR PRODUCT NIMBLE AND EFFECTIVE
Step 1
As the construction of your MVP is coming along, you need to simultaneously determine your target audience. Right here, I see many companies

---

26 When you have more people in the team, it usually implies the necessity for a taller hierarchy. So more people can get promoted to managerial positions.

27 I am sure that fact that MVP also stands for Most Valuable Player is not lost on the product managers.

screwing up. I see way too many CEOs say that the whole world is their company's target audience. "This product is for everyone."

Here's what I have to say to them: there are very few products that all people on the planet can consume. Unless you're building bridges, mass-transit systems, or free-size ponchos, your product is not for everyone. You need to understand that even commonly used products like sneakers need to be tailored to different segments of users. This also involves tailored messaging, brand, and pricing strategies. One of the biggest reasons for a product gaining unnecessary weight is that people who are building the product don't know whom they are building it for. So they decide to take a shotgun approach and start putting in more and more features, with the hope that at least some features will resonate with somebody out there. The more specifically you define your target market, the more directly you can speak to them (37), and the more likely it is that you will only include features that resonate with just this market. If you don't get that, you're going to face a world of pain.

OK. Now that I've gotten that out of my system, let me reiterate Step 1. Determine your target audience. Done.

Step 2

Understand your target audience completely. This is not limited to a demographic level, but should be extended to a deep, psychographic level. You need to understand their every whim, what drives them, what influences their behavior, what colored underwear they prefer...Well, maybe not that, but basically, everything there is to know about them.[28] Understanding your users from a psychographic level will help you understand why they behave the way they behave. You'll see their underlying

---

28 Don't take underwear lightly. Many studies have been done about the intimate relationship between people and their underwear (sorry...couldn't resist the pun!). One study revealed that about 10 percent of men actually have their mothers-in-law buy their underwear for them! And a significant chunk of the underwear bought by the mothers-in-law are...you guessed it! Tighty whities! (38)

motivations, and the link between their motivations and their behavior. It goes back to all the good stuff I talk about in chapter 7.

———

> One of the biggest reasons for a product gaining unnecessary weight is that people who are building the product don't know whom they are building it for.

Step 3
Focus on their core product needs. Do this from the perspective of the jobs-to-be-done theory (39). According to this, instead of segmenting your customers by demographics, if you understand your customers by the jobs they are trying to accomplish, you will be able to develop products that are more tailored to their needs, and you will be better able to predict what your customers will or will not buy. In other words, strive to understand what tasks they need to do instead of thinking about what features you'll be building for them. Pick just the core needs. Build your product around these needs. *Just* these needs. Nothing more.

Step 4
OK. So here's where you are so far. You now have an in-depth knowledge of your customers' persona. You also have an in-depth knowledge of how they work and what they need. You have a prioritized list of their top needs. Armed with all this knowledge, you can start to translate these needs into product features. You can do this by hypothesizing what kind of feature will resonate with them the most and then engage in an iterative process whereby you design and test with your target market repeatedly until you have a prototype that's fully fleshed out. The product you build for them should only have core features that meet their core needs. It should be a lightweight product that can do a few things very well.

Example:

Let's assume you're building an email application (why you'd do that this late in the twenty-first century is beyond me, but that's what you're insisting on building, so I'm going to go along with it). Let's say your research revealed these top five needs:

1. Ability to create a message
2. Ability to send and receive email
3. Ability to open and read a mail you receive
4. Ability to store emails the way you want
5. Ability to search for and find a mail at a later time

That's it. Make sure you build an app that does these five things. That is your minimum viable product.[29] According to Eric Ries, there's a little more to it. But what I have outlined will give you a general idea.

Now that you have a minimum viable product, how do you develop this product scrum after scrum? How do you keep yourself from fattening it with more and more features?

Again, let's look at research for this.

First off, there are two things you need to focus on in every scrum iteration (use research to guide you in what to prioritize, and how[30])—

1. Continuously improve your MVP to make the existing features more effective and less buggy. That's right. I'm telling you to do

---

29 At the time of writing this book, there's an image going around online that purports to explain what a minimum viable product should look like. For the love of all things holy, don't adopt that as the product philosophy in your company. According to the image, if you're looking to build a car, the minimum viable product is a skateboard. Seriously? If you find any sense in that, please tell me what you're smoking. I'd love a whiff!

30 Research can help you obtain a list of most important tasks that your customers absolutely need to do. Translate these tasks into features. Prioritize them based on things like urgency, frequency of usage, and criticality. Once you obtain the prioritized list of features, work with product managers in translating them into scrum stories and slot them into appropriate backlogs.

more work only on refining existing features. What I'm *not* telling you is to add more features.

2. Add new features only under three conditions:

    a) You have research data that proves that the new feature is absolutely required.

    b) You have had a fantastic, creative idea that you think will be a game changer. Test this idea out before you implement it in the product. Either way, make sure that any new feature is well tested and experimented on before it makes its way in the product. This one is so important (40) I'm going to say it again—run experiments with a small subset of real users to see how they react to this new feature before you launch it. By experiment, I don't mean usability tests. All of that should be done in the prototyping stage of the product itself. What I'm talking about is actually building a lean version of the feature and testing it with a small subset of your target market. If you don't do this, you're going to be sorry. Just as you would be stupid to go into battle with an untested weapon, it would be equally stupid to go into the market with an untested feature.

    c) When you add a new feature, consider removing one from the existing set. Yes, I went there! I talked about removing a feature! This is the most painful thing imaginable, but that's the only way you'll keep your product light. Again, use solid research data (and product analytics) to help you decide what feature you'll remove. Caveat: don't remove any feature from your core product (the top five features that constituted your MVP). Your product will collapse if you do that. Always remove the more superficial features.

You will now have a product that is light, but powerful. A light product will be able to effectively stand up to competition. Keep in mind that competition these days is more likely to come in the form of equally simple, but well—made products from small startups, and less likely in the form of overweight products from giant enterprises.

And there you have it, folks: the secret to building a product that stays simple, nimble and effective!

11

A researcher walks into a bar, and nobody cares. Ha ha!

The impact of company culture on research success

"We have a research team that conducted formative research on our product. The team worked really hard and came up with some good insights. Unfortunately, none of those were communicated to us. We had to end up designing the product without the benefit of any research. I really don't know why they even did research!"

—DESIGNER FROM A FORTUNE 500 COMPANY WITH A CHARISMATIC, CELEBRITY CEO

"The saddest thing in life is wasted talent."

—FROM THE MOVIE *A BRONX TALE*

Company culture is an interesting phenomenon. It is one of those things that a researcher can do little to control but still has a significant bearing on the researcher's success.

I want to be clear that what I'm talking about is a subset of the company culture. I am not talking about things like "learning from failure" or "a culture of innovation" or "integrity always," although things like that indirectly impact research (sort of). I am talking about elements of culture that have a direct bearing on the success of research in the organization. Let's start with the component I'd like to call "hunger for research."

User research is not like most other functional areas in the company. It has certain peculiarities. First off, there's the size of the research team. Even very big companies (with tens of thousands of employees) have very small research teams (tens of researchers, at best). Typical ratios of researchers to nonresearchers in most companies tend to range from 1:100 to 1:1,000 or even worse. I'll talk more about this in chapter 14.

For these "lone ranger" researchers to be successful, they need support from nonresearchers. They need allies from other functional areas. And they need buy-in at an executive level. In addition to this, they also need a research head to serve as a voice of the researchers. I've talked more about this in chapter 14 on how the research team should be organized. The most successful model has a research head, someone who can champion user research at an executive level. But first, for all these things to happen, the company needs to have a hunger for research across the board.

This hunger for research should permeate the organization—from an executive level all the way down to the trenches. Executives should be open to making decisions based on good, robust data. And so should people at the grassroots level of the organization. More importantly, the recipients of the research data should be open to changing their viewpoints in the face of contradictory research findings. This is one of the hardest challenges that researchers face.

Dave Morris is a well-known guru of improvisation. In a TEDx Talk, he defines listening as the willingness of a person to change (41). That is a powerful concept. See, often, people say they are listening when in reality they are not! Think about a recent experience in your own life when someone was talking to you and you were nodding along. I bet two things were happening when you were "listening." First, your mind was wandering.

The level of attention you were paying to the talker kept fluctuating. One instant you were paying close attention to the talker, and the next, you were thinking about something totally different, something like—"I wonder what's for dinner tonight. I haven't had tacos in a while. But I think we're out of salsa and black beans. I don't know if I have the time to do a quick grocery stop on my way home...." You revert your attention back to the talker to see if he is saying something that would necessitate a response from you. Not yet? Where were you? Ah...tacos..."Wait! Maybe I could just have a quesadilla instead. I do have all that cheese sitting in the fridge...." Then you check in with the talker again.

And here's the second thing you do. You wait for the talker to take a pause so you can interject with "Really? That's amazing! I'm so happy for you!" The talker is happy to hear that. He thanks you and then proceeds to whip out his smartphone so he can show you pictures of the thing he has been talking about. Where were you? Right, cheese in the fridge...

Listening is hard. Listening to a researcher is even harder. The thing that makes it so tricky for people to be open to research is that researchers do something that people in other functional areas don't. They challenge assumptions and force the recipients of research to question their thinking. All product managers believe that they have a good sense of where the product is and where the future roadmap should be taking them. And rightly so. That's why they got hired in the first place. Then along comes a researcher. The product manager is thrilled at first that she now has an ally, someone who'll help her with customer inputs, someone who'll help her refine the product roadmap to make it even more effective. But then the researcher turns out to have a mind of his own.

See, the researcher's mandate is not to *validate* the product manager's assumptions and lend more support to them. The researcher's job is to provide reliable, accurate insights from the appropriate segment of people, whether they are customers or noncustomers. The insights that the researcher brings back may not validate the product manger's assumptions. In fact, they may even go against them and challenge the product manager to alter her roadmap.

And this is where the problem begins. If the product manager is the type of person who sees sense in the researcher's findings even if they go against her assumptions, then she has the arduous task of changing the way she thinks. Changing one's perceptions, assumptions, and viewpoints is actually hard and inconvenient, even if doing so would reap rich rewards in the long run. Very few people do this well. For the rest, it's like pulling teeth.

———

Listening to researchers is hard because they challenge assumptions and force the recipients of research to question their thinking.

There's also an ego component at play here. The product manager is seen as the custodian of the product's future. Who's this researcher to come by and challenge what the product manager is thinking? And these feelings are typically exacerbated when there is more than one product manager in the game, as is very often the case. Now two or more people have to agree that they should be changing the product direction based on the researcher's findings.

The tensions at play pose some pretty hard challenges for the researcher. For starters, this significantly influences the manner in which the product manager chooses to engage with the researcher. This may have a bearing on the extent of research that the researcher is "allowed" to conduct. Unfortunately, in a lot of companies, the stakeholders don't even risk giving the researcher the power to significantly influence the product roadmap. Most of the research is just relegated to usability testing, nothing more. There is no request for exploratory (or generative) research, period. If the researcher goes rogue and decides to do some generative research, that's fine by the stakeholder team. No one's going to do anything about those findings anyway!

Another area that the tensions between researchers and stakeholders could impact is the timing of research. As I have mentioned before, timing is key to research. Research is useless if the findings come too late. I've personally been in many situations when the stakeholders conveniently "forget" to inform me of significant changes in the product roadmap, both with regard to timing and scope. As a result, on more than one occasion I have proudly come back with some awesome research findings, only to be told, "You did an incredible job. But we have kind of moved away from that direction in our product plans now. However, customer feedback is always important, and your research findings will be of great value regardless." Yeah, right!

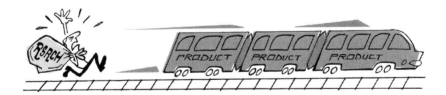

How do you make sure you time your study right? By being an integral part of the team. By this I mean being a part of every crucial meeting and even some hallway conversations. Most importantly, you do this by developing a rapport with the other people in the team so that they respect you enough to keep you involved where it matters. Research is not just about running studies. It's about building relationships with people—so that you matter to them, so that they take you seriously enough to do something about what you're telling them.

Regardless of how much research is done, and the kind of research (evaluative or generative) that is done, research findings in most companies are accepted at a very superficial level. Most changes are made at a "usability" level in the UI, and not at a functional level. It's very hard for research to get its voice heard in any other condition, even if all the researchers try their hardest. Someone should be ready to receive all their research energy, otherwise it will just get dissipated in a vacuum.

———

Research is not just about running studies. It's also about building relationships with people, so that they take you seriously enough to do something about what you're telling them.

So what other traits go hand in hand with research hunger and the willingness to listen?

At the risk of sounding idealistic, I'm going to say that another key quality that defines a research culture is humility. I don't go by the dictionary definition of humility; I define it as the ability to say "I don't know." I believe that in the age of aggressive corporate culture that pervades everything around us, these are the three hardest words in the English language.

Now, is there any company where humility is one of the core values and is lived well across the whole company, where every single stakeholder is hungry for good data, where researchers are in constant demand and all key decisions across all functional areas are driven by data?

Turns out, such a company don't exist! Granted, in every company there are a few pockets where somebody in a leadership role really believes in the value of research-driven decision-making. And such leaders may also be fortunate enough to have a bunch of product managers, engineers, and designers working for them who also place an emphasis on good research. And when the stars align, a lucky researcher gets to work with them, and you have a real-life fairy-tale situation on our hands where the birds are always singing and rainbows shoot out of unicorns' butts.

But such situations are hard to come by. Such teams are hard to come by, especially when we place so much emphasis on reward systems that value the individual and not the team. When individuals start competing for reward and recognition, they stop playing for their teams and start playing for themselves. Just like in baseball, where the batter still runs even though he knows he's going to be out, but does it anyway because his team member (and therefore his team) will get to score a home run, we need people who are willing to prioritize their team and the product they're building above themselves. This again comes back to the sense of humility, a feeling that the team is larger than each individual who's part of it.

So let me sum things up. Research is successful when there's a hunger for data across the organization. For such hunger to exist, the culture should encourage humility where people are not punished for saying "I don't know," but instead are encouraged to ask questions and look for answers. The culture should foster the willingness to listen and to change, where notions, no matter how dear, can be can be challenged without fear of repercussion.

PLAYING WITH POLITICS

2007. A major tech company in the Bay Area. A warm summer afternoon. I remember this day like it was yesterday. I was minding my own business working on a usability report. I did a lot of those—I had to. Some of them were over fifty pages long. No one ever read them. *No one.*

———

Hunger for research, the humility to say "I don't know," and the willingness to listen are the three characteristics that determine the culture where research can succeed.

Anyway, I digress. A research manager from the CRM team approached me. The fact that he was even talking to me was strange. Five user researchers at various levels of seniority reported to him. Yet he came to me. He wanted me to run a study on CRM. I told him I had virtually no experience in that domain, and inquired why he hadn't asked one of his own researchers to run the study. He said he was coming to me as I had the right experience and skills to run this study, and that no one in his team had the knowledge of methods or the skill set to run it.

I knew he was full of it. It was just a simple usability test. Anyone on his team could have easily done it. The plot thickened.

Apparently, a VP of product management of CRM had approached him about a particular set of features that were slated to appear in the upcoming release of the product. The VP wanted the features to be released. But other, equally powerful stakeholders did not. They felt that the features would not have the "wow" factor that the VP dreamed they would have. In fact, contrary to the VP's expectations, the consensus was that the features would muddle an already overcomplicated product. Everyone decided that user research was the tiebreaker. But it wasn't as simple as it sounded. The VP had something more in mind. Something more devious. He actually wanted the user research to demonstrate that users had no problems understanding and working with the features. Furthermore, he wanted research to *prove* that the features were essential to the users and helped them solve real problems. The kindly UX manager knew that this was dirty, and ever so graciously wanted me to run the study instead of someone from his own team!

I ran the study for him. Except I didn't give him the results he asked for. I gave him the real results from the tests: very few features were ready for release. More importantly, the users struggled to even interpret them, much less be fascinated by them. The UX manager did not like it. Nor did the VP. But as I found out later, they ended up doctoring my report, made a few strategic changes, and used it to launch the next version of the product, with the feature set intact.

Politics. It's a dirty word. Some companies don't even use the word, as it is considered taboo. A big company in Mountain View, California, in fact uses the words "relationship management" to describe navigating around politics. Why is that? Why are companies so afraid of even talking about politics? It's because politics is powerful. People who are good at playing politics become power centers of the company, and they don't want their success to be attributed to their ability at "relationship management." They want to be seen as honest, hardworking people, traversing the straight and narrow with integrity and purity of heart. They don't want to be seen as the jerks they really are. And once in a while, their paths will cross the user researcher's.

If you're a user researcher, how are you going to deal with it? To answer that question, you need to understand who you really are and where your values lie. I'm not going to lecture you about playing politics in your office. If you work for a company where the only way to climb the corporate ladder is by playing dirty politics, then by all means do so. But know this. When you corrupt your studies to appease others, you are no longer worthy of being called a scientist. When your integrity is suspect, it casts aspersions on your ability to honestly represent the customer. This is detrimental to yourself, your team, and eventually your company. When you signed up for the career of a user researcher, you made certain promises to yourself (or you should have). One of them is to treat data with respect, and to never compromise on the integrity of data collection and handling. Even if your career depends on it.

If you can handle that, then be a researcher. If you are the kind of person who wants to reach the highest echelons of your company at any cost, then user research is not for you. User researchers seldom make it to the top. Most end their careers at a director level at best. Very few become VPs. Very few. Be prepared for that. And with that, I'm going to get off this chapter. I really don't care for politics that much.

12

Some are born smart. Some achieve smartness. Others hire researchers (but don't pay them a whole lot)

All about hiring researchers

"Researchers are so boring. I wonder how people can hang out with them. Thankfully, you don't have to like the people you work with."

—DESIGN MANAGER ABOUT THE RESEARCHERS REPORTING TO HER

I live and work in the Bay Area of California. Silicon Valley. The hotbed of technology. Other than in the military, user research has arguably evolved more in Silicon Valley than anywhere else in the world. You'd think companies here would have figured out how to build the right user-research team, right? Wrong! It's a constant struggle in almost every company to figure out what the ideal research team should look like. Every company comes up with its own formula for this. Some work—for a while at least. Others fail right out the door. Even in the case when companies claim that their research teams work, the situation is so far from ideal that it's laughable. Why is it so difficult to build the right research team? For part of the answer, let's look at what happens when it comes to hiring researchers.

In most companies, research is somewhat of an afterthought. When planning for the next quarter, or year, how many companies do you feel really go, "First thing we need to do is set some money aside to hire some badass researchers"? I have to say, not a whole lot. In most cases, the budget for hiring is usually allocated first for the operations people, the ones that actually build stuff (like engineers in a product-manufacturing company). Then come the product managers, the strategists and roadmap builders. Then come the designers, the salespeople, marketing people…. What about the researchers?

To this, people at most companies would say, "Wait! Didn't I say 'product managers' and 'designers'? Aren't they the people who work with some sort of user data anyway? Shouldn't they be doing the research? Hey, guess what, we already have researchers! No need to hire anyone who actually goes by the job title of 'researcher.' Heck, what does a researcher even do that a smart designer or product manager doesn't? End of story." In essence, it is a fundamental lack of knowledge of what a seasoned user researcher brings to the table that keeps companies from even looking for them.

How do nonresearchers see researchers?

Over the years, I have seen five broad personas into which researchers are classified. Sadly, I don't think any of these personas will make the researchers very happy. Even more sad—there's a hint of truth to these categories. In fact, more than just a hint. Let's look at these personas, shall we?

To start with, there's the **Parrot**.

The parrot is great at meeting with customers and recording conversations. She has a lot of enthusiasm—all of it genuine. She excels at setting up research sessions in the blink of an eye. She is a great note taker, and a very good communicator too.

But what exactly is she communicating? After coming back from a research study, the parrot quickly writes up everything the customers said. And she shares all these notes with all the stakeholders.

Her notes are detailed. They are multicolored. The questions she asked are in red. The answers from customers are in blue. They have timestamps on them, so that you know exactly when the question was asked. She has pretty much transcribed every single word the customer said. She has also taken pains to highlight key customer quotes with a yellow background. They stand out and are easy to spot when glancing through. And oh look!—next to each important quote she has placed links to video clips of her participants speaking too! How awesome is that! She makes sure to share all the notes with all the stakeholders. She even schedules a presentation where she conveys all the information she has gathered to all the main stakeholders. She has prioritized the list of customer quotes so that the most important ones are at the very top.

Two weeks later, she sees that not much has happened since her presentation. When she talks to some stakeholders, the feedback is not very kind. It never has been for her.

Here's what they observed: In essence, she has repeated all the things the customers said. That's it. Nothing more. What's missing? There are no insights being derived. And without insights, there is nothing to act on. No recommendations. It's really up to the product and development teams to figure out insights and decide on what to do with them. And they do just that—except people start coming up with their own insights and their own interpretations. And it's chaotic with no definite call to action.

Soon, her study is forgotten. Her videos are still on the company's server somewhere. Nobody watched them.

Then there's the **Soothsayer**.

The soothsayer keeps things mysterious. His process is a veritable black box. Only he has the key to it. He has all these degrees in psychology. He is smart as a whip and has amazing insights into the inner workings of the human mind. He doesn't easily reveal his tricks. Even on the rare occasion when he does choose to reveal his method, there is an aura of mystery surrounding it all. Let's look at him when he's in action.

He seems to be conducting an interview with a customer. He has a list of questions that he keeps referring to. Granted, almost all the questions came from a product manager. But it must take an incredible amount of skill and training to ask those questions. He doesn't let anyone else do it. If a designer is watching the session and needs to ask for clarification, she cannot simply ask the question directly. She needs to write the question down on a sticky note and pass it to the soothsayer. The soothsayer, in his infinite wisdom, will determine when and how the question will be asked. Sometimes, he may even deem the designer's question unworthy of asking.

But the soothsayer is kind and benevolent. Today, at the very end of the session, when the customer is getting ready to wrap up and leave, the soothsayer turns to the designer and lets her question the customer directly! The designer, eternally thankful and giddy with excitement, asks two questions. The questions the designer asks seem pretty spot on—*to the naïve designer*! Not to the soothsayer, who shakes his head and, with a smile reminiscent of a sensei looking down at his floundering protégée, kindly rephrases the question and re-asks it to the customer. He then turns to the designer and whispers in her ear, "That is a leading question." The designer is ashamed. How could she even think of playing in the same field as the Great One? She makes a note to herself—she's not going to be asking questions anymore. Never ever. As long as she draws breath.

Next up is the **Salesman**.

The salesman is always busy. He keeps going out in the field and meeting with all these customers "in their habitat," as he phrases it. Not many people are privy to his project plans. He rarely shares his study proposals. But he does solicit questions from all the stakeholders. No one knows exactly what he does

with those questions. Not many people are invited to attend his sessions. He must be doing something really, really awesome all the time. After each field visit, he comes back, confident and bold—a man who knows what he's doing. They say he does "behavioral research." He gets into the core of the issue—he knows the truth underlying it all. At least he certainly looks like it.

Every time he winds up with a study, he organizes these big meetings—four-hour workshops with stakeholders. What does he do in these workshops? He shares his brilliant insights. The first thirty minutes of each workshop is devoted to him. The plan is that everyone first listens to his insights and then starts working on "how might we" exercises—coming up with ideas on how to "activate" those insights into product. He steps up to the whiteboard, all eyes riveted on him. He opens with a flourish.

He starts by describing the purpose of the study, and goes into the methodology used to gather data. When he is convinced that he has kept the audience waiting long enough, he presents his first insight.

"The main reason that fewer people are using our web app is…"—he pauses for effect—"…is that our customers are increasingly moving to mobile devices. People prefer to do things on the move. They need information at their fingertips. The name of the game…"—he pauses again—"…is immediacy"! He looks proudly around at the poor souls lapping up every word he says. He goes on talking for another hour. It's OK if he runs over the allocated time. Research is important. He is important.

Had he stayed back after the workshop (which ended surprisingly early—apparently all the PMs had a meeting they had forgotten about, and they hurried out halfway through the workshop), he would have heard the lead PM mutter to the designer in the hallway, "Next time, we do our own research. Even we can provide cheap, obvious 'insights' that can be gathered from anywhere. How much did we end up spending on this joker's project again?"

Then, how can we forget—the **Usability Tester**.

The usability tester is probably the most famous of all the researcher archetypes. It's not hard to guess what the usability tester does. She runs usability tests.

But as it turns out, she needs a lot of help running them.

For some reason, even though she has a master's degree in a relevant field, the usability tester is mind-numbingly incapable of doing much work by herself. Like a toddler who has stepped in poop, she needs to be constantly monitored and led carefully through every step.

To start with, she needs to be told by others what needs to be researched. The most important thing the researcher brings to the table, the ability to ask tough questions, is missing in the usability tester. The PMs and designers ask all the important questions.

So what value does the usability tester bring to the table?

The usability tester determines what kind of prototype is going to be tested and the personas it is going to be tested with. Then she recruits the participants. No, no, no…actually, that's not true. First off, she is blissfully unaware that such a prototype even exists. She has been conveniently excluded from all product-planning and design-review meetings. The designer hands the prototype to the usability tester after a whole bunch of people have determined that it is ready to be tested. Also, in many companies, the usability tester doesn't do any participant recruiting herself. She submits her request for participants along with a screener (which needs to be vetted by product management) to a recruiter, who recruits and schedules the users.

So what value does the usability tester bring? Let's start again.

The usability tester composes and owns the test script—the most important component of the study—uh, in the sense that a valet "owns" the Porsche dropped off by its owner at the entrance of the casino. The valet gets to drive it to the parking lot and even take a couple of selfies in it, but the real owner can step in and take it all away at any time. In a similar manner, the two main components of the test script—the scenario and the tasks—are both really controlled by the product manager and designer.

Let's try again.

In the event she doesn't have a note taker…Oh wait—she does have a note taker. The observers are taking notes. They really determine what's worth recording and what's not. Plus, the session videos are being recorded on GoToMeeting.

Oh, come on! There's got to be something she does. The company pays her a lot of money. What does she do?

Oh. I get it! She runs the test!

Wellllll…To be fair, she does ask questions and administer tasks according to the test script. But the observers keep interrupting her. Either they keep pinging her questions to ask via text messages, or even worse, jump right in without invitation and start asking questions to the participant directly, totally unsettling the participant and the usability tester and screwing up the whole study.

So maybe the usability tester wows everyone with her analysis skills and blows everyone away with her insights?

Hmmmm…As it turns out, there's not a whole lot of analysis involved. She does have to watch hours of recordings again. It turns out most observers did very little note taking. But how can that be? She saw them typing a lot of stuff when the test was going on. Turns out what they were typing wasn't notes from the session; maybe they were typing out emails, or they were chatting with their colleagues, or maybe they were on Facebook. She will never know.

Anyway, she watches all the videos again. She identifies usability issues and records them on a Google spreadsheet. She has a column for each participant and a list of issues along the rows. For each issue, she puts a neat little "X" under the participant who had that issue. She then sums up all the issues under clear headings (in a different font and in different-colored cells). She has even, in her delightfully naïve way, calculated time on task and task-completion rate. Bless her heart!

Then she schedules a findings presentation with all the fourteen stake-holders. She originally wanted to do a half-day workshop, but the PM advised her that won't be necessary. A one-hour presentation will be more than suffi-cient. She has prepared a nifty keynote slide deck that she preshared with all the invitees in the calendar invite. That way, people will have already become familiarized with the key findings before the meeting starts, and during the presentation she can go beyond what the slides say, talking about acting on the findings. She has scheduled the presentation on a Friday morning at 10:00 a.m. That's when the most stakeholders are most likely to be free. She has booked a nice big conference room well ahead of time (after all, a lot of people are going to be coming). And my word—has she brought in Krispy Kreme doughnuts and Peet's coffee? Yes, she has, the darling!

It's Friday at 10.15 a.m. There are two people in the conference room. One is our usability tester. The other is a design intern who is new to the company. No one knows how the intern ended up in a meeting only meant for key stakeholders. The intern is twenty-two years old, fresh out of college, and is really, really, really excited to be there and can't wait to see the findings!

As it turns out, most of the stakeholders work from home on Fridays. Some of them have dialed in, but they have all muted themselves. It's hard for the usability tester to know if they are even there anymore.

Anyway, she goes through the presentation with very few interruptions, and finishes in twenty minutes. She asks the people dialed in if they have any questions. The silence is deafening. She asks again, this time reminding everyone to unmute themselves. After what seems like an eternity, the product manager's voice comes on the conference console: "No questions here. That was an awesome study. Thank you so much for all your efforts!"

"Sure, no problem," trills the usability tester. "Is there anything—"

She is cut off by the console announcing that the PM has left the conference. She looks around, as if seeking some solace from the empty chairs around her. She is greeted by the gorgeous, doll-like, Bambi eyes of

the intern, who is full of admiration for the usability tester. This is the intern's first conference with a real adult. It's sooo exciting!

And finally, we have the **Hydra**.

The mythical hydra has many heads—the world's first multitasker. Actually, the underworld's first…but let's not split hairs about it. All hydra researchers work incredibly hard. They're always busy and adopt multiple roles within the company. They are well-meaning, but in a desperate drive to create impact, they take on way too much. And in the process, they tend to lose track of what they should and should not be doing. Their efficiency suffers, and, tragically, so does their impact.

Hydras are eternally busy. They communicate with stakeholders, constantly looking for new research ideas. Their biggest disadvantage is that they don't know how to say no. They are always willing to help, and in the process, they end up getting overwhelmed and overworked. They find it hard to figure out what projects they should take on and what they shouldn't.

Something like this is what's going on in a typical hydra's head at any given moment: "OK. I need to do this major project that will help determine what kind of users are most likely to visit our website. But I'm not sure if anyone has committed resources to act on my findings. I need to start by pegging down some deadlines. Then, there are these three smaller projects—actually two. The third one's not even worth calling a project. But I have committed to doing them all. And then what about recruiting? I have to do that myself. And the scheduling—for all my projects. And then, there are the workshops, and the two presentations I have committed to doing. And what's this—oh crap! I forgot to send out the incentives to the participants in my last study. Great! One of participants happens to be the CFO's personal friend, and he has just emailed me a terse reminder, copying the CFO. That son of a bitch! And I really can't do any recruiting for Project Two unless I figure out the personas, and I can't do that because the lead PM's on vacation…and what's that? I have to participate in a two-hour design review. When? Now? *You've got to be kidding me!*"

Oh, if only they had someone who would guide them! As a matter of fact, there are people who want to do just that—guide a hydra. They are designers, product managers, and developers. And here's the advice each of them would give to a hydra: "My project has CEO-level visibility. I suggest you drop everything else and focus on this." Uh, that helps!

And there you have it: the most common researcher personas, as others see them. At some time or another, every researcher would have belonged to at least one (if not a combination) of these personas. In general, the researcher community has not done a stellar job creating an identity for themselves and differentiating themselves from others (nonresearchers) in the company who do research. It's actually a very hard thing to do. There are two reasons for this. One is the very nature of user research. The field of research is something that is hard to articulate. Even seasoned researchers have told me they find their job hard to explain to a layperson. But research, when done well, can have an incredible impact on the company. It's kind of like sex: you won't get it unless you have experienced it!

Now, here's the second reason. Unlike engineering or sales, research is something that anyone in a company can take a stab at, and in many instances, they actually do. Not surprisingly, some people can even claim a certain level of success at it. So naturally, the big question is, "Why even bother to hire researchers, when we are already doing it?" A lot of the purist researchers out there may not like this, but there are a number of very successful researchers out there who don't have formal college degrees, and have really just learned on the job.

Then again, there are a lot of good researchers who came up the "right" way—went to school, got relevant degrees in cognitive psychology, HCI, human factors, etc. And they are very successful too. So the big question is, if you're hiring a researcher, which is better? Hire researchers with formal training, or "grow" them from within the organization?

In general, the researcher community has not done a stellar job creating an identity for themselves.

FORMALLY TRAINED VS. ORGANICALLY GROWN RESEARCHERS

Before you make a decision, let's take a look at the typical path of how a researcher organically evolves within an organization. I'll illustrate this with a story.

Lacy Wierdqueries is a product manager. She has an interdisciplinary bachelor's degree in economics and political science. She is just as likely to have been a marketer, designer, or document writer. She has been working for about two years now at Spit&Shake, a customer-relationship-management consultancy. For the past few months, Lacy has been working on understanding what exactly clients are looking for when they say they need a CRM solution. It seems to her that every customer is unique, with unique needs. How might she tailor some solutions that can be used by multiple customers? Are there any patterns across customers that she can leverage?

As part of her journey, Lacy starts interviewing a bunch of customers. In the beginning, she is a bit skeptical. How can she be sure she's asking the right questions? And what part of the customer's answer should she really pay attention to? Every bit of what the customer says seems so important! But as time passes, she discovers that she's actually getting good at it, and more importantly, she has started to enjoy the creative process involved in understanding her team's needs, crafting questions, and getting to the heart of the customer's concerns. She also enjoys learning about people, their work habits and behaviors. She is beginning to spend nearly half of her time just talking to customers and analyzing the notes and videos she has been making.

At this point, she starts thinking seriously about making research the biggest part of her job content. She talks to her manager, who has also been observing the change in her. From here, the logical next step is to change her job title. Two year later, she is now the senior user researcher at her company. Her manager's even talking about letting her lead her own team in due course. It would be a shame if Spit&Shake had not let Lacy choose this career path.

Now that we've seen a typical example of how researchers evolve by themselves in a company, let's get back to our initial topic. What should you do? Hire a researcher with a formal degree and experience, or let a researcher organically evolve within your own company? Let's compare the pros and cons of both approaches.

Formally trained researchers
Pros

- They come with great knowledge and experience with methods.
- They have more people to train them, as usually technical-domain experts tend to outnumber user researchers.
- Not every product will need a dedicated researcher all year long. Since the researcher is not tied to any single domain, he can easily move from one product space to another. The organically evolved researcher will usually end up being stuck in the domain in which he has expertise.

Cons

- They don't have domain expertise. And the learning curve needs to be pretty steep, because without domain expertise, they can only be moderately effective at best. Sadly, a lot of researchers take a long time to acquire domain expertise. Many don't go far in this area at all.
- It's really hard for researchers to have an "in" with the product, design, or development teams. They will always tend to remain second-class citizens.

Organically evolved researchers
Pros

- They come with great knowledge and expertise in their domain. But they lack research expertise or knowledge. They need to learn on the job.
- In general, it's easier to learn to do good research than it is to acquire good domain expertise. Even the most veteran researchers in most companies have only a cursory domain knowledge. I have seen many marketers, product managers, designers, and even a few engineers make a successful transition to user research. But rarely have I seen a user researcher make the transition to product

management, marketing, or development. Some researchers, however, have managed to become fairly successful designers.

- Since they already belong to PM or dev teams, they have an "in" into these teams. They have a higher chance of being more effective because a) they are part of the team they are trying to influence, and b) they speak the language of their coworkers and know both sides of the story. Oftentimes, you see researchers get frustrated when a team doesn't implement their recommendations, because they are not fully aware of the obstacles that team may be facing. That will not be a problem for organically evolved researchers, as they know the inner workings of the teams they originally came from.

Cons

- It's a bit hard to find mentors in user research in the company. This is a serious problem, because so many organically evolved researchers learn from sources that are less than authentic and don't know what they don't know.
- They don't tend to ask the right questions, and their implementation of methods is shoddy. Many of them tend to stay at the same level of incompetence for years. It's painful to watch.

As you can see, the decision to "grow" vs. "hire" is not an easy one to make. While on the surface it seems like a good idea to organically grow researchers, the mentoring thing becomes a big issue. Many companies have self-made researchers who, after a few years, actually start taking leadership roles in research. They guide their company in user research and are considered experts. They train others, present at conferences, and write blogs. They become opinion leaders and have huge Twitter followings. All the while, they don't have a goddamn clue what research really is.

On the other hand, the company can end up hiring these stuffy, formally trained user researchers with their PhDs and their holier-than-thou attitudes. They don't have any true friends anywhere in the company and find it incredibly hard to get anyone to act on their findings. Because let's face it—having friends in the right places helps more than having a PhD!

So what's the solution? It's a case-by-case thing. When you don't have too many research projects, complex exploratory research projects, or long-term research projects, and all your research is primarily usability testing and concept validations...it's OK to have some organically grown researchers handle those projects. Probably better that way.

When you have complex research needs, when you need somebody to ask tough questions and provide data— and evidence—driven guidance, when you think you are going to have a steady stream of research projects and need someone who really knows her stuff, then a formally trained researcher is the way to go.

QUALITIES OF A GOOD RESEARCHER

Regardless of who you go with, there are a few qualities you absolutely need in a researcher. No compromise here. When I say "qualities," I am going a bit further than things like ability to be a team player, integrity, etc. I am talking about some qualities very specific to researchers. Qualities like…

Having friends in the right places helps more than having a PhD.

Empathy

Empathy refers to the ability to put yourself in the shoes of others and feel what they feel. The "others" could be internal team members or customers. Researchers should be able to home in on specific behaviors and clearly postulate why such behaviors occur. They should also be able to translate their observations into clear, actionable insights that other team members could use. And the icing on the cake—they should also help others develop empathy.

Storytelling ability
Stories impact emotions. They spark imagination and make complex ideas come to life. Stories have the power to change minds. Most importantly, stories instill passion. Researchers can collect data and analyze it. They can decipher numbers and make sense of them. But unless they are able to bring these numbers to life by providing rich stories that underlie them, it is very hard for people (including themselves) to relate to what their customers are facing. The ability to tell stories goes hand in hand with the ability to create empathy for the customer.

Communication and collaboration (people skills)
Researchers should involve all key stakeholders in research, right from the get-go. Their communication should be timely and relevant. They should have the ability to tailor their communication style depending on who they are speaking with. Like a good joke, a lot of communication is all about timing and the punch line. Researchers should know what to say, whom to address, and when they should address them. Coupled with this is their ability to work together. At the pain of repeating myself, I once again insist on this fact—researchers will be successful only if they involve other people in their processes. Collaboration is vital to researchers' success.

Humility
I've talked about it in my chapter on company culture (chapter 11). Researchers should be humble enough to say "I don't know" when they really don't. We don't want to hire fraudsters who claim to know every-thing. In fact, researchers should be proud of saying "I don't know." Every time they say this, they are actually giving themselves an opportunity to learn something new.

Curiosity and the desire to satisfy it

They should be eager to find answers to their questions. They should be motivated to learn new things. Constantly. Regardless of how experienced they are. When the researcher's curiosity dies, a part of the researcher dies with it.

Energy and enthusiasm

Researchers should not be jaded, but instead display real enthusiasm in tackling challenges. You want to hire people who welcome challenges and rise to the occasion. They should genuinely be interested in how their work impacts the company.

Culture fit

Culture is a tough one. There are two aspects to it. One aspect deals with how the culture of the company is conducive to good research being conducted in the company. The other aspect deals with how the researchers can fit into a company's culture. I talked about the first aspect in chapter 11. I'm talking about the second aspect here. Let's examine it deeper.

Define the culture of your company in a few sentences. Go on. Try it. I can wait.

Was it easy? More importantly, do you think it captures the essence of your company and what it means to work in it?

When you were defining your company's culture, I hope you didn't confuse your culture with your company's values. Values are easy to remember. They're probably written on a wall somewhere by the lobby. Culture has to do with the DNA of the company. Values represent ideals. Culture represents the reality.[31] Let's say you did come up with a reasonably accurate description of your culture. By using your description, are you able to say whether you are a good fit in your company or not?

---

31 For example, a company can have "integrity" and "always put your customer first" as two of its *values*. But it could have a *culture* characterized by employees always backstabbing each other and coming up with new ways to stick it to the customer.

As if this weren't complex enough, the culture fit while assessing a researcher is even more tricky. This is because while researchers should embody the company's culture, they should also be a bit nonconformist at the same time. They should be able to go against the tide and sometimes be the only voice of reason in a room full of opinionated stakeholders. Unless the company's culture values people who stand up for what they believe in, the researchers are kind of screwed, don't you think?

The culture fit is a huge problem when it comes to researchers. I have unfortunately witnessed multiple researchers who ended up losing their job because they were deemed to not be a "culture fit," while they were actually the exact thing their job demanded! Understand this aspect well before you hire a researcher.

Independent thinkers
You can't hand-hold your researchers. You shouldn't. Researchers should be capable of making key decisions and acting on them. This doesn't mean they should work in silos. Far from it. It means they should be independent thinkers who are also humble enough to ask for help when they need it, and who know when to involve whom. They should be OK working as an army of one occasionally.

Chutzpah, in a nice way
You want your researchers to be a little badass. To show courage and conviction and just a little gall. It takes a bit of nerve to tell a whole team of smart product managers and designers that their idea will not pan out with customers. But they also need to combine chutzpah with tact and delicacy. That's the sweet spot!

Passion–not for the product, but for research
Finally, there's one aspect that we haven't covered yet. Passion. Not for research; that has to be there. But passion for the product itself.

Consider this—let's say you're working for a Facebook gaming company. Your company is insanely famous for one particular game. You are looking to expand your research team and are conducting job interviews. After an exhaustive screening process, two candidates stand out, Alex and Brooke. Both have about five years of experience and are similar in every way except for one crucial difference. Alex is a consummate gamer himself. He is very passionate about the game that your company makes. In fact, he happens to be one of the top players of the game. Brooke, on the other hand, has never played the game before. In fact, she is not even a gamer. Who would you hire for your team? Alex or Brooke?

Alex, right? It should be a no-brainer. Why would you even consider Brooke?

Yeah…except for one thing. Hiring Alex goes against one of the basic tenets of being an effective researcher.

In my short little section on biases in chapter 8, I was talking about how you should guard yourself against biases, and about how it's not always easy to even know when you may be biased. The biases kind of creep up on you, and unbeknownst to you, completely screw up your analysis.

Now tell me this: if you are an avid gamer of the very game that you are conducting research on, how on earth are you expected to be unbiased? You need to literally get out of your mind and body to see things objectively and rationally (in other words, scientifically). And I'm no doctor, but getting out one's body and mind, and still being alive, is kind of impossible.

And I am not the only person who says this (not the bit about getting out of the body, but about distancing yourself from your product). Martin Lindstrom, the #1 brand genius and author of one of my favorite books, *Small Data*, says the same thing (42). Martin, who is Danish by birth, describes himself as an outsider to most of the world. In fact, he talks about how he has come up with innovative brand strategies not in spite of being an outsider, but because of it. In his words, "familiarity, in fact, is at best counterproductive, and at worst, paralyzing."

He goes on to give an example of a situation when Pepsi asked him help them improve public perception. He felt that having been a Pepsi drinker and having been exposed to all its advertising and presence in his everyday life compromised him. He was too familiar with the brand and the product. He had no frame of reference. He couldn't think straight, or get inspired. In short, he says in his book, "I couldn't do my job."

In order to distance himself from Pepsi, he actually stopped drinking it, in spite of the fact that he ended up going through something akin to withdrawal symptoms! He found that after six weeks of abstinence from Pepsi, he was finally able to function as a dispassionate researcher.

So, there you have it. Hire Brooke.

And when you do research yourself, you should strive to become more like Brooke. You need to distance yourself from the product, and more importantly you need to *not* become one of the users you are going to be conducting research on.

———

You need to distance yourself from the product and *not* become one of the users you are going to be conducting research on.

13

Aren't researchers afraid of heights? Should they be climbing ladders?

Setting the researcher's career path

"I'm sick and tired of being called a senior researcher. I want to get promoted at least once before I retire!"

—A USER RESEARCHER WITH SEVENTEEN YEARS OF EXPERI-
ENCE AT AN ENTERPRISE SOFTWARE COMPANY

"You know, you've pretty much reached the end of the road."

—A DEIGN MANAGER TO A PRINCIPAL RESEARCHER REPORT-
ING TO HER

We all want to grow in our organizations, regardless of what we do. Defining a career path for any given job type is essential in every company. It demonstrates that the company cares for its employees and rewards good work. It also gives employees a feeling that they have better things to look forward to in the company. It gives them a goal to strive toward. Linking the career ladder with pay hikes and more perks is an added incentive.

Career paths are reflective of the company culture and where the company is at any given time. More traditional, established companies tend to have the more structured, ladderlike career paths. The job titles in each path are also more formally defined. Larger companies also tend to have longer ladders with more rungs.

There are two reasons for this. First, these companies have more employees, which necessitates more managers and more levels of managers to make sure that each manager has a reasonable number of direct reports. Second, companies tend to create fluffy, unnecessary job titles like senior manager, lead researcher, senior director, etc. just to keep the employees motivated[32]—to make them feel like they got promoted, even if they didn't really get promoted. Oftentimes, the "senior" designation means absolutely nothing. The job content doesn't change one bit. The employee just gets a small bump in pay, and maybe a few more RSUs, and that's it. But it keeps the employees from complaining that they were not recognized. They did get a promotion, did they not? Nobody cares that the job title didn't mean anything.

With that introduction, let's examine two of the most common ladders for the researcher. These ladders are synthesized from career paths of ten Bay Area companies. Each of these are medium-sized companies or big enterprises.

THE TYPICAL IC PATH

The first, more common path is the independent contributor (IC) path. It typically has about six levels.

---

32 One of my friends was a principle engineer in a large company. He was really looking forward to his next promotion, which according to his career ladder, would be to manager. "Not so fast," said his company. They created a new job title for him. It was between principle engineer and manager. The title? Senior principle engineer!

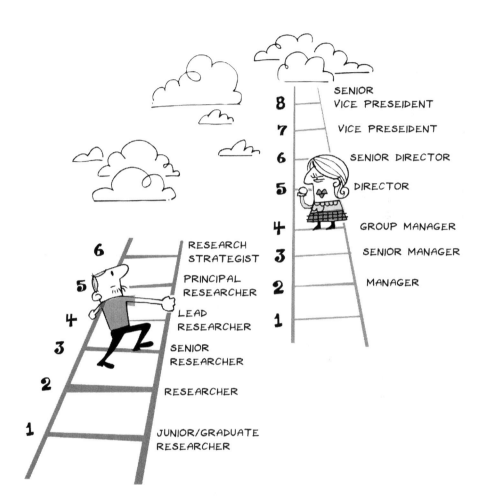

Level 1

Junior (graduate) researcher (some companies have two levels here)— They are usually fresh out of school, or intern-level folks. In some cases, they could even be part time. They typically aid as note takers in more complex studies, or run small usability tests on their own.

Level 2
Researcher—Standard workhorse. Usually have a couple of years of experience under their belt. For some reason, most of them come with master's degrees. That's too much if you ask me. A good bachelor's degree will do for most of the commonly available researcher roles.

Level 3
Senior researcher—Five years of experience (or way more, depending on the company). I have seen researchers with more than fifteen years of experience at the senior level. I think that's a little sad, and it starts getting into some of the broader issues related to how the researchers are viewed in their company.

Level 4
Lead researcher—This is kind of a hybrid level. In many companies, the leads also manage some junior researchers.

Level 5
Principal researcher—The craft leaders. They set up things like best practices that are followed by all other researchers. Their work usually has company-wide impact.

Level 6
Something funky above principal (like a research strategist, architect, or something)—They usually look after very high-level strategic stuff. Their work has company-wide impact at a very high, strategic level.

That's it!

And then there's the managerial path:

THE TYPICAL MANAGERIAL PATH
Even though I called it a "common" managerial path, it's actually a lot less common than the IC path. You just don't find that many researcher-managers in the wild.

Level 1

This is a level that is usually below manager (like a lead researcher)—The researcher here has been deemed good enough to lead a team, but not good enough to be called a manager yet. So he or she is asked to lead a small team while still doing a lot of IC-level work simultaneously.

Level 2

Manager—The standard workhorse in this ladder. Most research managers oversee a small team of researchers. They usually work with stakeholders to get projects for their team members to work on. In some cases, managers take on some of the more challenging research assignments themselves.

Level 3

Senior manager—A manager who does well for a period of time is usually promoted to be a senior researcher. As far as job content goes, most companies haven't decided on the differences between a manager and a senior manager. They are usually the exact same job, with the senior having a bit more experience.

Level 4

Something above senior (like principal manager or group manager)—Again, this is another fluffy rung whose sole purpose is to promote a senior who has been at that level for a while.

Level 5

Director—Most researchers tend to end their careers at this level (if they are lucky enough to even rise to this level). A research director's primary job is to interface with senior members of the stakeholder teams. The director often serves as the voice of the research community in the company and is responsible for setting up the researchers' path to success.

Level 6

Senior director—Not very common. A director who does his or her job well is promoted to the level of a senior director. Job content-wise, there isn't much difference between a director and a senior director. Another fluffy level, if you ask me.

Level 7

Vice president—Very rare for researchers. I have only come across a handful of researchers who made the VP level in midsize-to-large companies. Typically, when researchers become VP, they start managing teams of people other than just researchers. They generally manage entire UX teams.

Level 8

Senior VP or executive—It's mind-numbingly rare for a researcher to reach this level. This is also another fluffy level created to promote VPs and make them feel better about themselves.

Level 9

Head unicorn in charge of all the rainbows—Just kidding! I don't know any researcher who made it past a senior or executive VP level in a non-research consultancy company—such researchers only exist in an imaginary land. If you know of real-life researchers at this level, shoot them and mount their heads above your fireplace. They will fetch a lot of money in the black market.

What of researchers in nontraditional companies? Oh, that's really hard to nail down. Each company can come up with their own choice of levels and their own job titles for each level. While some companies still go with the more traditional job titles, others create job titles such as master of disaster, catalyst, chief cheerleader, and ambassador of buzz (43). And that goes for researchers too. The problem here is that if the job titles are nonstandard, the gaps between different job levels are nonstandard and almost completely arbitrary too. The growth path is entirely dependent on the company. Most nonstandard companies are also usually smaller. There are not many researchers in such companies anyway. So "growth" is a pretty loosely defined term in such companies.

Now how does a researcher grow in more traditional companies? As it turns out, it's not as easy as in other functional areas. Why? To answer this question, let's look at the obstacles that researchers face in their efforts to get promoted.

Probably the biggest thing in the way of researchers getting promoted are the researchers themselves. In chapter 12, we looked at how researchers are commonly perceived. We even created "personas" of such researchers. As I mentioned earlier, there's truth in each of those personas, although most researchers would probably feel that they don't belong to any of them. Of course, nobody conforms to any one persona in its entirety. But whether researchers like it or not, they do end up conforming to one, or a combination of the categories.

In this section, we are not going to just stop at these personas. We are going to go deeper—into the psyche of the researchers. We are going to uncover some of the key reasons a lot of researchers don't make it beyond a middle-management level in their entire careers. It all has to do with something I'd like to call "the invisible researcher." Here's the story of one such researcher.

THE INVISIBLE RESEARCHER

Ethereal Vapors had been a researcher for eight months. She loves her current job as an associate researcher at OhWhatever, a company that makes apps for teenagers. A fresh graduate, Ethereal considered herself lucky to have found a job at such an amazing company. Rumor had it that the company would go IPO soon. An independent firm had valued OhWhatever at a gazillion bajillion dollars.

Probably the biggest thing in the way of researchers getting promoted are the researchers themselves.

Ethereal lived within a twenty-minute walk of her company, and she took full advantage of it both ways, to and from work. Not many people get a chance to live a walking distance away from their workplace, and Ethereal knew that. She paid an obscene rent at her studio apartment just for that privilege.

One evening, Ethereal was walking home after a tiring day at work. She was hurrying up, as it looked as if it might start raining any minute. As she neared her house, she noticed an injured chameleon lying by a bush along the sidewalk. Being the kind woman that she was, Ethereal picked up the reptile and gingerly held the chameleon in her hands, wondering what was wrong with it. At that precise moment, lightning struck Ethereal and the chameleon in her hand. In that blinding moment, the powers of the chameleon miraculously transferred to Ethereal. But she didn't know that. She had passed out. It took a few weeks for Ethereal to recover. But she was a trooper and pulled through. Eventually, she got back to her work as a researcher at OhWhatever. She kept herself busy going about her business, juggling different studies, analyzing them, preparing deliverables, making presentations, running workshops. You know—doing the things that researchers are wont to do. She did a pretty good job at this too, and had a fair amount of success in impacting the product roadmap.

One day, her team wanted to celebrate their recent success and head out to a bar for a happy hour. They invited everyone who had contributed to the project. Everyone but Ethereal. You see, just as they were deciding whom to invite, Ethereal had disappeared, blending perfectly into her surroundings, like the chameleon she had been trying to rescue a few weeks ago.

A few weeks later, when the company CEO was launching the product at a conference, the people who had contributed to the success of the product were asked to stand and be recognized by the crowd. Ethereal disappeared again.

It didn't take long for Ethereal to realize that on that fateful night, the lightning that struck her left her with a unique but unfortunate superpower. Every time she was up for recognition for her work, she would become invisible. Every time there was a critical meeting about product strategy, she was overlooked, as no one could see her. Ethereal was shocked at this discovery of her superpower. Plus, she was incredibly saddened by it. In fact, her one constant struggle was to be seen, to be heard, to be acknowledged as a person who made a meaningful contribution to the product. But she didn't have a choice. And she couldn't control her special abilities, no matter how hard she tried.

Many years have passed since that fateful stormy night. Ethereal moved on to another company, but her superpowers remain strong. Even to this day, whenever an executive wants to reward somebody for doing amazing work on a product, or even take the team out to a celebratory lunch, they always forget Ethereal. She turns invisible just at the key moment.

As it turns out, Ethereal is not the only person afflicted with the "gift" of invisibility. A lot of researchers remain invisible, sometimes throughout their careers. Researchers tend to be introverts or are borderline introverts. The nature of research is to introspect, ask questions, ponder. And many deep thinkers tend to be introversive. This doesn't mean that extroverts fail at being researchers. All I'm saying is that the probability that researchers are introverts is much higher than the probability that they are extroverts.

Unfortunately for them, today's work environment is designed to favor extroverts. People need to sell themselves all the time. They need to make noise, evangelize, and make sure everyone knows about them. They also need to belong to a team, which is very hard for researchers, especially as they don't have strength in numbers. Which brings me to the next reason why they are not promoted…

THE DEARTH OF RESEARCHERS

The next obstacle to a researcher climbing the ladder is the small number of researchers in the company—far too low to even be recognized as a separate team in most organizations. To make things more challenging, most projects have just one researcher. They have an army of product managers, engineers, and designers…but only one researcher. Also, most researchers end up leaving the project once they hand over findings from their research. So they really don't have much claim over the finished product.

The number of researchers in a company also affects the managerial ladder in a much more pronounced way. You can't manage researchers if you don't have any researchers to manage. The managerial ladder for researchers is usually pretty short in most companies. The lucky researchers who make director usually end up managing the entire group of researchers in a large division, or even the entire company. Even they typically have only two rungs of researchers under them.

Then there is also the issue of deliverables. Researchers' deliverables are usually not the finalized designs. So when an executive wants to look at the work the whole team is doing, no one bothers to show him or her the researcher's deliverables. Instead, what's put on display are designs. Designs are sexy. Designs are cool. Research? Not so much.

Now let's look at the other end of the spectrum. Consider an area like marketing or sales. Most marketers tend to be extroverts. They like promoting themselves, and being professionals, they are actually good at it! Plus—and I grudgingly admit this—they even dress better! The rest of the company falls in the middle of the introvert/extrovert spectrum. So where does it leave the researchers?

Unfortunately for a lot of researchers, today's work environment is designed to favor extroverts.

Summing up, we have a range of introverts, very small in number overall, who tend to be loners as far as their functional area goes, and don't stay on for the entire duration of the project, and are usually not tied to any other functional area. None of these augurs well for career growth and development. Most companies don't even have dedicated career ladders for researchers. They either mimic a designer ladder, or worse, an engineer's career ladder. Experience and craft leadership don't translate the same way in research as in engineering or product management. But that's the best most companies can do. The researchers just have to live with it. Or they have to fight for their place in the hierarchy.

RESEARCHERS GO AGAINST THE GRAIN

I'm going to have to admit this. Researchers sometimes rain on other people's parades. The researcher's job is to uncover things that the company should fix. As a result, all researchers invariably end up focusing on the negative. When they present their findings, they usually pepper them with quotes from participants, almost all of them highlighting some problem or the other. In contrast, marketers always focus on the positive. When they solicit customer quotes, they always look for quotes that are buoyant and energetic. This sort of thing puts the researcher in a negative light. People don't even want to hang out with these Negative Nellies. So why on earth would they feel like promoting them?

NONRESEARCHERS DON'T UNDERSTAND RESEARCH OR KNOW HOW TO EVALUATE ITS EFFECTIVENESS

As a result, one of two things can happen. A fairly inexperienced researcher can keep getting promoted over and over. None of the others understand research, and they feel that every time a researcher comes back with some findings, they need to reward her! They don't even know what a real insight should look like. They are happy that someone is talking to customers and coming back with "findings." And the person does a good job presenting her work. That's all a researcher should do, right? Plus, no one really built a researcher career ladder. Who wants to deal with the one moping researcher in the team? Best way to keep her quiet is to keep promoting her!

The other side of this situation is terrible. No one understands research. And they want to err on the safe side, by not promoting the researcher at all, or at least not often enough. You'll see a researcher barely make "senior" after many, many years. In the meantime, many nonresearcher colleagues have made director and have already bought that big house in the suburbs the researcher can only dream about! Then those nonre- searchers have the gall to retire early and buy their daughters ponies for their birthdays.

SO WHAT DOES A RESEARCHER HAVE TO DO TO GET PROMOTED AROUND HERE?

Some of this is in the hands of the researchers themselves. They need to understand the challenges they are facing—challenges that result from the intrinsic nature of their field to challenges that are a result of their own personality. They can't just keep doing their work and hoping they'll be noticed. Researchers need to do a bit more. They need to know how to market themselves and their craft. They need to keep making noise. Keep publishing something or other in their company's intranet. Keep reminding people that they exist, and that they are working on something or the other. They also need to make their research relevant and demonstrate their success visibly.

There's an easy way to tell if they're being valued. They get more requests from different corners of their division (or even company, if the company is small enough) for research projects. People start inviting them into meetings that they were previously not privy to. They start being considered part of the bigger team. Of course, the company's culture and the manager's awareness of the power of research form the two other crucial components that determine whether a researcher is recognized and promoted.

So I have gone over the culture part. Let me now talk about how the manager can recognize good research work and reward the researcher who does it.

As a manager, you need to be looking at the three things a researcher should absolutely be doing: asking the right questions, coming up with insights from data, and making these insights actionable. In this case, here's how you should evaluate their levels.

THE IDEAL CAREER LADDER FOR RESEARCHERS – THE IC LEVEL
Level 1
The researcher mostly does what she is told to do. She asks some basic questions to get her project going. Most of these questions are hardly provocative or far-reaching. Her application of methods is fairly rigorous and conforms to what she has learned in textbooks or in the classroom. She produces a good, clean report with all the necessary details without being too verbose, and is able to make a decent presentation of

her findings. She does not come up with groundbreaking insights because that's not what her study is all about. She does work with her colleagues in product/design/etc. to make sure the findings are incorporated in the product. She doesn't drive any decisions. She merely helps substantiate the decisions others make with her data.

————

> As a manager, you need to be looking at the three things a researcher should be doing: asking the right questions, coming up with insights from data, and making these insights actionable.

Level 2
This researcher asks some far-reaching questions regarding product direction, personas, etc. There is some independent thinking. More importantly, he starts anticipating the future of the product. He talks about different product scenarios and how they might evolve in different conditions. Depending on how complex the product is, the insights he uncovers would impact either an entire set of features and functionality or even the whole product itself. Of course, he is able to conduct rigorous research and is well versed in all the methods. (This goes without saying, and applies to all levels of the researcher ladder. So I won't be mentioning this for the subsequent rungs.)

Level 3
For the most part, this researcher is an independent thinker. She also proactively starts questioning a lot of things. She comes up with her own research roadmap and conducts research that impacts the long-term future of the whole product. She is a leader. She is capable of walking into a room full of skeptics and pivoting their thinking process. She knows the power of data-driven decision-making and is able to reach even the

hardest critics about its effectiveness (whether they agree with her asser-tions is another matter entirely[33]). She is also a good mentor and teacher.

Level 4

Everything in level 3, plus the researcher conducts research that influences the entire product roadmap for multiple products and works with every-one in the product team. He focuses all his energies on doing challenging exploratory work. He continues to mentor people, but at a much higher level.

Level 5

Everything in level 4, pus this researcher conducts research that influences decisions by key organizations in the company, like product, marketing, etc. The questions she tackles are broader, much more long term, and far reaching. She probably hasn't run a usability test in a long, long time. She is also too busy to mentor newbies. She has a single-minded focus: taking the teams depending on her to the next level.

Level 6

The highest level in the company for a researcher. He conducts research that changes the direction of the whole company. He works and influ-ences senior leadership. He also becomes an advisor to senior executives on key decisions. He has in-depth knowledge of what's out there beyond the walls of his company. In addition to this, he also understands internal

---

33 As I have mentioned previously, not everyone sees research the same way, and certainly not everyone will agree with the insights a researcher comes up with. This could be due to a variety of reasons, ranging from the company culture to individual personalities, office poli-tics, etc. The manager needs to be very aware of the environment in which the researcher is working. Especially at higher levels in the organization, not every failure of a researcher can be attributed to the researcher alone. The manager needs to work with the managers of other teams to make sure that research success is as much a responsibility of other teams as it is the responsibility of the researcher. This piece of the puzzle is often missing in most organizations.

limitations and knows exactly what has to be done within the company to succeed. People like him are rare.

Finally, apart from the levels outlined above, there are three areas in which a researcher should be well versed. They are detailed below. The higher up the ladder a researcher goes, the more proficient in these three areas the researcher should be.

1. Knowledge and solid application of methods
2. Knowledge of how to run research
   a. Asking the right questions
   b. Identifying the right focus areas
   c. Working with the right people and managing relationships
   d. Respecting rigor
   e. Managing budgets
   f. Communicating well
   g. Dealing positively with different kinds of stakeholders
   h. Thirsting for knowledge
   i. Showing eternal curiosity
   j. Deriving insights
   k. Turning these insights into actionable product/design decisions
3. Ability to train others in conducting research

WHAT ABOUT THE IDEAL MANAGERIAL LADDER FOR A RESEARCHER?

In the rare event a researcher is called upon to manage a team, there is also a managerial ladder she could be climbing. This ladder is actually quite similar to the managerial ladder in any other functional area, so there's no need to outline the different rungs here.

14

Flipping out on the crazy pendulum of uncertainty

Placing the research team in the company

"Hey, I never said I don't like researchers. I just feel that they don't belong in my team."

—EXECUTIVE VICE PRESIDENT, MARKETING, IN A LARGE CLOUD-COMPUTING COMPANY

"I know you feel like you've been moved around a lot. But believe me, you're right where you need to be now. I'll make sure you get to do the best work of your careers."

—DIRECTOR OF UX TO SEVEN RESEARCHERS WHO JUST GOT MOVED INTO HER TEAM. WITHIN SIX MONTHS, SIX OF THE SEVEN RESEARCHERS HAD QUIT THEIR JOBS. TWO MONTHS AFTER THEY QUIT, THE DIRECTOR GOT PROMOTED TO VICE PRESIDENT.

I've already mentioned this a couple of times before. But I need to say it again to set the context for this chapter. In any company, the research team is usually one of the smallest teams around. This could be because…

1. Companies always tend to underinvest in research.
2. There is a perception that there really isn't that much research work around. Most companies tend to use research to validate designs—so a lot of research tends to get concentrated at just one part of the product life cycle. Besides, if all researchers do is validation, then they can easily be replaced by designers or product managers anyway.
3. Oftentimes, a designer or product manager who has run a study on usertesting.com thinks of himself or herself as a researcher and precludes the company from hiring real researchers.
4. Research takes much less time if viewed as a percentage of overall product development time. So many companies don't have enough going on to keep the researchers busy on a regular basis.

For perspective, consider this: One of the Bay Area's biggest software companies has well over 65,000 employees. Yet the whole company just has a handful of researchers—fewer than twenty! One of the largest employers in San Francisco has over 15,000 employees, out of whom twenty-two are user researchers. And one of the largest companies in the world, a company that has been at the forefront of technology for over a hundred years now, has over 360,000 employees, but less than 0.1 percent of them are user researchers.

The list goes on.…

Given the small number of researchers, a company is left with some interesting options on how to organize these researchers. There are two key areas of consideration here. First, where in the organization will the research team be located? Second, how will the research team itself be organized within the group it finds itself in? There are multiple options for both, and of course, each option has pros and cons. Let's look at them.

LOCATION OF THE USER RESEARCH TEAM

For starters, let's look at organizations where user research is more widely accepted. In such organizations, the following are some of the more common places where you would find a research team.

The design team

This is the most common configuration. The research team is part of an overall UX team (or the design team, as it is commonly called). The UX team is usually led by a leader who comes with a background in design. The team itself is made up of a mix of designers and researchers. The ratio of researchers to designers is roughly in the range of 1:8 to 1:10. In other words, there are roughly eight to ten designers for every researcher. Do I applaud this ratio? Probably not. But that's the nature of reality. Let's go with it for now.[34]

What are the pros and cons of being embedded in a design team? I have to say if a company has a separate design team whose head reports to the CEO, they are actually in a fairly good place. In many cases, designers are the closest partners a researcher ends up having in an organization. But this also implies that most research is done in parallel with design phases. In other words, the most support that a researcher gets is during initial design, wireframing, and subsequent design validation. So the UX team has the opportunity of producing good, data-driven designs. But things get a little challenging after that.

---

34 Interestingly enough, once the number of UXers reaches one hundred or so, companies start calling themselves "design led"! They think they have now become Apple. The head of the team thinks he is Steve Jobs (and for some reason, it's always a "he"). Some even start dressing like him!

Remember why I wrote this book? It is because so little research eventually makes it into the final product. And part of the problem is that the impact of research begins and ends with design. Once the designs are handed off to product management, it's touch and go in most organizations.

There is another critical reason why research suffers under design. It's a mismatch of core personality types. Researchers and designers are entirely different kinds of human beings. Their personalities are different. They even look, dress, and act different. But tempted as I am to launch into a narrative about the personality differences between researchers and designers, that's not what I want to talk about now. What I want to talk about concerns something that every researcher will face while working in a design team—the design manager.

It is a widely held belief that research can be a subsidiary of design. And why not? As I mentioned before, designers are usually the researcher's closest associates. And a lot of user research deals with user interfaces that are very much in the wheelhouse of design. Some companies go so far as to call user research "design research" because that's what it is—it is research that informs design. (I don't condone it, by the way, I think it severely limits the capability of research and, frankly, is pretty annoying.) It should come as no surprise, then, that a designer is often put in charge of research (and almost never the other way around).

And here comes the problem—design and research are two vastly different disciplines. Clumping them together under a design manager demonstrates a fundamentally flawed assumption that research and design are somehow the same. The fact that some designers also do research doesn't make them researchers in any sense of the word. It's like calling me a doctor just because I administered first-aid when my son scraped his knee.

The fundamental difference between design and research lies in how the practitioners of the two disciplines think. Design at its heart is a creative discipline. Research at its heart is a scientific discipline. The difference between design and research is the same as the difference between an artist and a scientist. When you get a scientist to report to an artist, there is a very good chance the scientist is going to be unhappy, and more importantly, very likely unsuccessful. What's worse, the artist is going to be looking for deliverables that appeal to other artists, but the scientist is on a totally different page, and struggles with a dichotomy. On the one hand, she needs to produce a deliverable that actually impacts the product. On the other, the same deliverable should be visually appealing to the designers (and to her manager). The second part, unfortunately often takes precedence, because it is more important to keep your manager happy than to have actual product impact.

Clumping research and design together under a design manager demonstrates a fundamentally flawed assumption that they are somehow the same.

I have come across multiple instances where researchers have been praised by their design managers. In some cases, they have even been promoted. I looked at the work and found one striking thing the researchers had in common—their deliverables. They had the right content for the most part, but the quality of work they did was not that much better than that of other researchers (who were not promoted). Then it struck me! They had the most sophisticated-looking deliverables I've ever seen from a researcher! When I asked them how they acquired the skills to produce such deliverables, I was quite surprised by the answer. They actually had visual designers help them with beautifying their deliverables!

Now, whenever I brought this topic up with design managers, they almost always said, "That's hogwash!" They said they didn't want pretty deliverables. They wanted functional deliverables. The format of the deliverables, or their visual appeal, didn't matter to them at all. Yet time and time again, the reports that were featured as "best in class" were stunningly pretty, and clearly had tons of input from someone well versed in design. As validation, I heard this from a designer friend of mine who works at a major social-media company in the Bay Area: "I am currently helping our lead researcher make her presentation pretty. We have found that if the presentation is really slick, she has a better chance of getting a much bigger audience to listen to her findings. In fact, all the researchers who are successful in making a presentation at the team's all-staff have one thing in common—they have a designer craft their presentation." So much for functional presentations!

In a design team, the researcher will always be a second-class citizen. That's the hard truth. If you don't believe it, look at the managers in the design team. A design manager always gets to manage researchers. But a researcher managing a team of designers? Now that's crazy talk!

Now for some other places you can find a research team.

Research and development

The R and D team itself is either a stand-alone team reporting up to a chief technology officer or a product head or a development head. Regardless, it's not a bad idea for a user-research team to be embedded within R and D. Trust me, it could be much worse. R and D, especially if it's of a reasonably good size, actually does have a considerable impact on product development. But not a whole lot of companies have teams calling themselves R and D. In most cases, the research and development work is folded somewhere in the deep recesses of product management. I will talk about what it means for research to be a part of product management as we go along.

Before that, let's look at the impact of having the user research team embedded in the marketing department.

Marketing

Yeah. This one's tricky. And there's one really big reason for this—marketing research. You see, most people are very familiar with marketing research.

But not a whole lot of them are familiar with user research. What is the difference between the two, and does it matter? Back in chapter 6, I vehemently stated that all that matters in any company is that they do good research and not worry about whether their research is called user research or marketing research. (If I recall correctly, I advised against being an "anal-retentive sourpuss," and to let the matter rest. I still stand by that.)

Unfortunately, not everyone thinks like I do, and the one time the distinction between marketing research and user research needs to be considered is when you locate the user-research team within the marketing division of your company. So, against my better judgment, I'm going to start talking about the definitions of marketing research and user research.

The American Marketing Association defines marketing research the following way:

> Marketing research is the function that links the consumer, customer, and public to the marketer through information—information used to identify and define marketing opportunities and problems; generate, refine, and evaluate marketing actions; monitor marketing performance; and improve understanding of marketing as a process. Marketing research specifies the information required to address these issues, designs the method for collecting information, manages and implements the data collection process, analyzes the results, and communicates the findings and their implications. (44)

And what is the definition of user research? I have already given this definition all the way back in chapter 1. *User research is the science that helps us understand the causes and manifestations of user behavior and the resulting interactions of users with their environment.* When you take a cursory look at the definitions for marketing research and user research, they seem significantly different. (Well, for one thing, the marketing-research definition has way more words than the user-research definition; it's from marketers, so what did you expect?)

But how does this pan out in practice? Let's see. Marketing research deals with the collection and management of information obtained from customers—information that deals with marketing opportunities and problems, and communicates this information back to the company. User research also collects information from customers and communicates it back to the company, albeit a different kind of information—this has more to do with mental models, usage patterns, behaviors, and pain points. But when you get into areas like pricing, purchasing, social interactions related to product, usage behavior, and attrition, you're getting into a pretty gray area. These are of interest to both marketing and product management, and any research insights in these areas would be valuable to both the teams.

More importantly, when dealing with such insights, companies really don't care about the distinction between where the research came from or, for that matter, who did that research. Which means, in the company's eyes, all research sources are the same. Now what does this mean for user research? From what I've seen, when user research reports to marketing, it tends to get lost, and in many cases, suffers an identity crisis. Most formally trained researchers (by this I mean people who have degrees related to some branch of psychology) would like to think they go deeper into people's minds than the average marketing researcher.

Marketing researchers, on the other hand, tend to feel that they are bringing in real data because they rely more on quantitative measure than the "touchy-feely" stuff user researchers rely on. There is no real solution to this problem except keeping user research from reporting to marketing. In chapter 6, I discussed how the two teams can work together. Just remember that they tend to work great together when one team doesn't report to the other!

Quality assurance

Why anyone would combine user research and QA is beyond me. But believe me, this has happened. I think it's mainly because they look at research as usability testing and QA as quality testing, and you have a common word there, "testing," and someone said, "You know what would be a great idea? Let's put them both together!" Not cool. By pairing QA and testing, what they are really saying is that user research is just another checkbox in a long list of things that need to happen before product launch. Again, not cool. I won't talk about this anymore, as even thinking about it pisses me off.

When dealing with insights, companies don't care about where the research came from or who did that research.

The web team

This is another weird place in the company where you can find user research. By making user research a part of the web team, the company has demonstrated that the only place where research can have any impact is on their website. This is OK if the company offers a web-based service and the website is the main channel of communication between the company and its customers. It's not OK if the company is a product company and the website is just one of the channels where the company does its sales. Then the user-research team will have no impact on the product. Why even bother having a user-research team if you're going to relegate all its activities to just the website of your company? Seriously, *why*?

All right, there is one more location for the user research team that I haven't talked about yet. This happens to be the location where I think research will have maximum impact. And that location is product management.

Product management

This is by far the best place for user research to be located, way better than the UX/design team. Product managers also tend to be product owners. They create the product roadmap and are responsible for the successful inclusion of key features in the product. There are endless articles and even books written about how researchers should work with the product team. But I am going a step further here. I'm saying that the best way to convince them is to join them.

Being embedded in a product team is really very good for researchers. They get a lot more exposure to every phase in the product roadmap. There is less chance of researchers being left out of crucial product-related discussions, as they are more likely to physically sit near the product managers. They are much closer to the action. Plus, they get to develop strong relationships with product managers, which comes in very handy during the uncomfortable phase of making sure which research findings make it into the product and which don't.

Of course, the researcher would have to end up reporting to a product manager. But that's no different from reporting to any other functional head. At least in this case, the researcher is reporting to someone who can actually impact the product!

Now that we have that part squared away, let's look at the next, troublesome question that every research team has to grapple with. How should the research team be structured?

HOW THE RESEARCH TEAM ITSELF IS ORGANIZED
Option 1. A centralized research team
Here's what it usually looks like.

There is someone at a director level leading the research team. Researchers at various levels (including a couple of research managers thrown in for good measure) report up to this director. The director in turn reports to a design head or an executive of sorts. That's it. All researchers are one small happy family.

How do these researchers engage with other teams? It's kind of an agency model. The team has a few choices here. A few researchers could be dedicated to specific product teams. These researchers might spend fairly long durations of time embedded within their team (a few months to even a few years). Then there are other researchers who could be fluttering in and out of smaller projects based on demand—spending anywhere from a few weeks to a few months per product. They could also be working on nonproduct research projects—like helping brand, marketing, customer support, etc. The researchers in this paradigm have a kind of dual-reporting format. They HR report to research managers or their research director. They also dotted-line report to the heads of the projects they are working for.

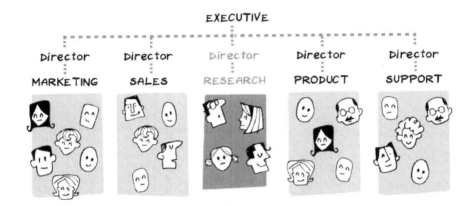

This kind of model has been proven to be one of the more sustainable models. For one thing, researchers get to hang out with other researchers and report to a manager who understands research. For another, they actually get to choose (at least on reasonable teams) the projects they get to work on, and if they don't like a project, no worries, it will all be over in a few weeks and they get to work on another project! They also have a director who represents them to the execs and serves as a voice of the researchers.

But there are also some disadvantages to this model. From a practical standpoint, the researchers end up having dual reporting structures. They HR report to their managers, but functionally report to product heads, or design heads in other teams. From a career-development perspective, such "agency researchers" could have a harder time moving up the ladder, as performance evaluations from the different dotted-line managers tend to be inconsistent. What's more, this dotted-line reporting keeps changing every time the researchers move from project to project. They really don't have the ability to build a strong relationship with any one team, as they are always viewed as transient. It's hard in such an environment to make a serious impact on the product-development process.

Option 2. A decentralized research team

In this scenario, the researchers don't report to a research head. There is no research head to report to. Instead, this organization is all about having researchers reporting to the manager of whatever design or product group they are working with for the most part. Some researchers support the product for all its research needs. Others could be scattered around the organization, reporting to entirely different functional heads. This actually seems intuitively a better way to inject research into the complete product ecosystem (including all its supporting groups). And there are many advantages to this sort of organization.

Primarily, researchers have the opportunity to get completely plugged into all the core divisions of the company. Since there are researchers embedded into product management as well, they can be part of all the crucial conversations and assist the team with its research needs through all stages of the product lifecycle. This becomes even more pronounced if the teams that the product researchers are working with follow an agile development process (like scrum). They can set up a regular cadence with their teams and make sure that the research insights keep coming in tandem with their team's sprints.

Incorporating research into agile development has posed many problems for researchers in the past. Most researcher methodologies and participant-recruitment processes traditionally followed a waterfall model. The problem with this kind of approach is that by the time the results of the study are ready to be shared, the team has moved on to other things, and the findings from the study just sit in a report somewhere collecting dust.

With most companies trying to move to a somewhat "agile" kind of model, they do these things called "sprints." I say "agile" and "sprints" in quotation marks because very few companies really follow the agile methodology. They are really somewhere along the spectrum between agile and waterfall. But whatever it is they do, two things are clear:

1. The team is trying to work faster.
2. There is less time for research.

So the closer the researcher is to the product team, the higher the possibility that the research can be plugged into everything that is going on and can actually slip in some research wherever possible. This model really cashes in on that advantage.

Having said that, how successful is this model? This model works pretty well at the outset. But over a period of time, a few problems begin to surface. These problems don't have much to do with the org structure per se, but more to do with the nature of the researchers and the managers they report to. If you haven't read about it already, take a look back at chapter 13. Researchers need to report to managers who understand research, and who understand the mentality and attitudes of researchers (they are a unique bunch, these researchers). Most product managers and designers don't go the extra mile to take this into account. The results could be pretty dismal for researchers. Their career ladder might be selected arbitrarily to reflect that of the other team members they are working with, and they could become isolated with very little access to other researchers in the company.[35]

SWINGING FROM ONE CRAZY POST TO ANOTHER

In case of Option 1 (the centrally organized research time), the big issue is that researchers tend to be far removed from product and are accused of not having enough impact on product because they are not embedded deeply enough in the team that makes all the decisions. In case of Option 2 (the decentralized model), the problem researchers face is that while they are well entrenched within the team they need to influence, they end up feeling lonely and disjointed, and may not experience their desired career growth because their managers don't quite get research.

Companies have come up with an incredibly stupid solution to solve this problem, a solution that can single-handedly spell the demise of research in those companies. I call it the Pendulum of Uncertainty. And the unwitting researchers get to swing on this pendulum from one post to another, just like crazy monkeys! Allow me to illustrate with a short story....

Koko Buttcheeks is a user researcher working in San Francisco at a fast-growing company that makes a mobile dating app for sixty-year-old widows with five children or more. When Koko joined two years ago, he was the first researcher in the company. For the past two years, he has been reporting to

---

35 In many companies, researchers try to remediate this situation by coming together in the form of an unofficial group. They set up monthly or biweekly meetings where they share each other's stories and pain points. They also use this to give the more junior researchers a chance to learn something from their senior counterparts. To some extent, this provides a way for researchers to talk to other like-minded individuals, and even advance their craft in the company a little bit, but, in the long run, this group meeting becomes "one more meeting I have to attend." I have witnessed that sometimes researchers also discover that their counterparts in other teams are doing much better than they are, which tends to make them feel even more depressed. So much for camaraderie!

Dave Swinger, a design manager who is awesome in every way imaginable (as design managers always are). Dave, in turn, reports to BJ, the head of design. Since Koko joined, Dave has hired three more researchers at different levels. The researchers have been following a centralized model where they all report to Dave, but with each researcher working on a different feature set of the app, like the age-verification feature for instance (people below sixty are not eligible), or the mandatory DNA-testing feature to verify that the children indeed belong to the mothers, as they claim. Life was awesome for two years, until one of the new researchers complains that she is not having enough impact on her feature. She laments that it's because she has little contact with her stakeholders, and she is not even invited to critical meetings where they make product decisions.

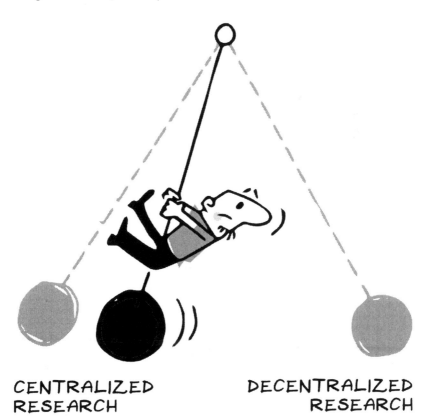

CENTRALIZED
RESEARCH

DECENTRALIZED
RESEARCH

Dave is not happy to hear this. He walks up to BJ and tells him that something needs to be done about it. BJ wastes no time. In the company's next all hands, he announces a change in the research organization. The researchers will no longer be centralized. They will, instead, report to the design heads for the different feature sets. This will solve all problems. Dave, who no longer has any researcher directly reporting to him, is given a raise and promoted to senior design manager to make him feel better. He does feel better.

A year passes. The number of researchers in the company has not grown at all. The design managers do a lot of hiring, but none of them hire any new researchers. They do hire a whole bunch of new designers, including a bald dude with a nose stud and some prison tattoos (all the designers think the tattoos make him look so hip and authentic!). Koko is concerned. Research has clearly taken a backseat. None of the researchers are happy. Some of them have updated their LinkedIn profiles and openly made it known that they are looking to leave the company.

Koko decides enough is enough. He has a heart-to-heart talk with BJ. BJ, ever the man of action, decides to do something about it. He announces another re-org. The researchers are reunited in a centralized team. Dave is put in charge of all the researchers again. He is also promoted to director of design research, as a reward for his initiative in making BJ aware of the problems in the research domain. Dave is happy. Dave also hires three more researchers. The new researchers report to the bald dude with the nose stud and tattoos, who is suddenly promoted to design manager. They could have reported to Koko, but then why would anyone report to a researcher?

———

The Pendulum of Uncertainty could single-handedly spell the demise of research in your company.

Another year passes. Koko is concerned that too many design and product decisions are being made with absolutely no research input. He has another heart-to-heart talk with BJ and Dave. The design heads know what is at fault. The researchers are all so centralized now. No one has any connection with the stakeholders from other teams. That's got to be it. At the next design all-hands, Vice President Dave has an announcement to make. Koko groans.

Koko's story is not unique. I myself have been in four companies where they do this crazy, insane pendulum swing from centralized research team to decentralized research team every once in a while. It is crazy, messed up, and can be considered the main reason why research fails. Oddly enough, the designer part of the UX team is never reorganized. The designers are always centralized and remain one big happy family!

What can be done about Koko's predicament? I might have a solution. A different way to organize the researchers. Here it comes.

Option 3. A mixed setup

The third option is really a combination of the first two options, hoping to gain all the advantages of the first two while doing away with some of their negative effects.

Here's how it works. The research team is broadly split into two parts—a centralized research team and a product research team. The members

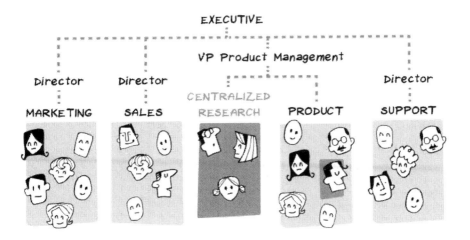

of the centralized team report up to a research head, who in turn reports to someone like the VP of product management. The members of the decentralized research team report to different heads of product management (I was going to say product-manager managers, but that would be awkward!).

The product researchers' jobs are well defined. They are very similar to those outlined in Option 2. They take care of all aspects of research for their respective product or product feature set. They are fully integrated in product planning and design. For complex products, there can be more than one product researcher sharing the research load.

The centralized researchers take care of cross-product initiatives, strategic research, as well as research in areas that are not product specific—such as customer support. They can also step in when the load on any one product researcher is unmanageable for a certain period of time. The centralized researchers would also follow a little more of the "agency" type model, as outlined in Option 1. They tend to be focused on some of the more vague, exploratory research—the kind that drives core decisions that have company-wide impact.

In order for this model to work and offset some of the cons of the first two options, there needs to be a close working relationship between the product researchers and the centralized researchers, even though both teams have different sets of managers.

How effective is this option? For one thing, this model has the potential to avoid the transient nature of research that Option 1 was plagued with. This model allows for researchers to be embedded into products, while allowing for some researchers to be dedicated to less-defined and temporary research projects. It also allows for researchers (at least some of them) to be collocated—solving for the "loneliness" issue that researchers in Option 2 tend to face. To make the model less rigid, it would be a good idea to let the researchers move from one team to another when it is right to do so.

So, is this the perfect model? I am not really sure we can label any model as "perfect." It is really a question of tailoring the best model to the situations at hand. For one thing, this model does require that there be a sizeable number of researchers; it obviously doesn't make sense when there are like two researchers in the entire company! This implies that the company is fairly large, so that it even needs two sets of researchers. Also, for there to be product researchers, the product lineup should be fairly complex.

For another, the success of this model depends heavily on the nature of interaction between the product and centralized research teams. Increased interactions will help the researchers share their workload better and deal with issues related to stress, loneliness, and the lack of attention paid to research.

In this chapter, we learned that where the research team is located and how it's organized has a pretty significant impact on how effective that research team would be. The research team is small and delicate. If you don't know how to handle it, you won't reap its benefits.

15

For the finale–Let's assess your net worth

Measuring the impact of research in terms of ROI

"It took us twelve years to get here. But for the first time ever, this year, I was no longer asked to provide ROI for UX research."

—VICE PRESIDENT OF USER EXPERIENCE AT A FORTUNE 500 COMPANY

At one point in time, the design team was reporting up to the chief marketing officer at one of the companies I worked for. Being a marketing guy, it was only natural that the CMO questioned the value of every component in his team. By value, I mean ROI.

Marketing has different divisions, from product marketing to event marketing, and from marketing research to brand management. Every single component of the team needs to justify its existence or risk getting laid off. That's the nature of things in many companies, especially in a field like marketing, where layoffs are incredibly common.

Now, every company has two kinds of teams.[36] There are teams whose value is immediately apparent, and there are teams whose value isn't.

---

36 This is the finale. I *have* to divide the world into "two kinds."

Engineering, product management, finance, and sales are in the former category. Marketing usually finds its place in the second category.

What the CMO failed to understand when he came up with the ROI mandate was that three things contribute to a well-made product: a healthy dose of creative design genius, excellent product-planning skills, and a good measure of user data collected through rigorous research. Ignoring any one of these could lead to any of the following: a) a really good-looking, aesthetically pleasing product that is almost unusable and impractical; b) a functionally robust and easy-to-use product that looks ugly and lacks proper affordances; or c) a good-looking, simple product that lacks a well-balanced feature set. And that comes with a set of high quality designers and product managers in addition to dedicated researchers.

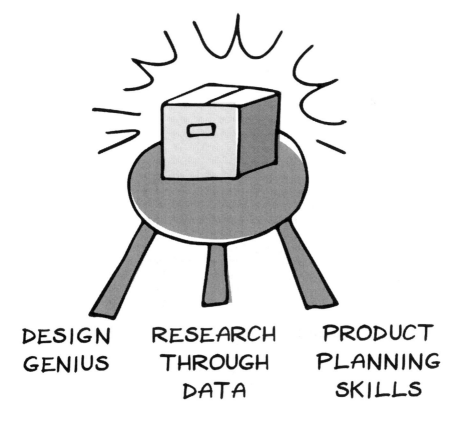

DESIGN
GENIUS

RESEARCH
THROUGH
DATA

PRODUCT
PLANNING
SKILLS

It goes without saying that of these three groups of people, the folks who are responsible for bringing good product planning and execution skills to the table, the product managers and engineers, are seldom asked to justify their keep. Everyone knows intuitively that good product-management teams and good engineering teams are vital to the success of the product. The other group of people—designers— also has a relatively easy job of convincing people of their importance because, by its very nature, most people can easily see the value of good design.

So, it came as no surprise that when design was asked to justify its existence, it easily stepped up to the challenge. Select designers showcased their skills. They made cool videos of futuristic versions of the product. And then there were the "real life" customer videos. They'd find customers who spoke about how the new user experience radically changed everything in their world and made them mind-numbingly successful in their businesses. There were posters of customer testimonials singing the praises of "well-designed" products stuck in prominent places within the company. Articles were written in famous people's blogs and hip magazines like *Fast Company* and *Wired* about how cool design is the most important thing in the world and about how "our company nails it." Designers also stood out visually, with swanky haircuts, tattoos, piercings, jeans rolled up to the ankles, and hipster beards. Design was cool. Designers were cool. They really didn't have to justify their existence. It was implicit. Even a fool could see product development was impossible without design. And no one would dare cut back on design. Not in Silicon Valley. Not in technology. Design was holy. It was Steve Jobs's domain. 'Nuff said.

When it came to research, however, it was a whole other story. As it turns out, it's pretty hard to demonstrate the value of research. For starters, there were the usual challenges mentioned in other parts of this book. Everyone could do research, the company already had a marketing research team, blah blah. You could counter it with all the objections I came up with earlier in the book, but that's not enough when it comes to showing ROI. That is because even if a product has benefitted from the best possible research, it is ultimately called a *well-**designed** product.* And two teams get credit for this—product management and design. Research merely *informs* them and *helps* them make good decisions. So the ROI of research is tied to the ROI of product management and design.

Then why is it even important to demonstrate the ROI of user research? And how do you even do it?

Before I answer these questions, I have to give you a disclaimer:

I think being asked to demonstrate the value of research is absolute baloney. If you are in a company where you are asked to justify why research is important, I'm sorry, my friend, but I have no better advice than to *leave the company and never come back.* Asking someone to demonstrate the value of research is the same as asking the person for the value of intelligent decision-making. Research helps you make intelligent decisions. If you value intelligent decisions (and I hope for your own sake that you do), then you should value everything that goes into making those decisions intelligent. Research is one of them. That said, let's get back to the task at hand—justifying the importance of research through the magic of ROI. Why do some companies insist on it?

Well, first off, there are stakeholders. Sadly, some of these idiots don't get the value of research. Even if they do, they may not get the value of *researchers* (especially in companies where the only thing a researcher does is usability testing). These stakeholders could hold the key to whether research succeeds in their company. So it is very important that some sort of ROI is demonstrated to them.

Directly tied to this is the issue of budgeting. If people who hold the purse strings are convinced about the value of research, they'll choose to allocate funding for research projects. This could include salaries for the researchers as well. So prove the ROI of the work you do, and keep your job. Makes sense from that standpoint.

But the real problem comes when you think about actually measuring it. The thing about ROI that you should be aware of is that the effectiveness of ROI varies depending on what you use it to measure. If you are using ROI to assess the impact of research on the company's overall revenue, that is going to be really difficult. Research is really one out of a million things that affect company revenue. And the credit for the revenue will go to the more powerful (tangible) departments.

———

Asking someone to demonstrate the value of research is the same as asking for the value of intelligent decision-making.

In order to get some sense of this ROI exercise, we would need to redefine ROI—redefine it in such a manner that the word "return" doesn't mean anything in monetary terms. And "investment" shouldn't be measured in terms of the dollar amount spent on research in a given time period, but rather in terms of the number of studies done, and even the type of studies conducted. They can always be tied back to dollar amounts at a later time.

For example, what is the "return" obtained when you run a concept test? To understand this, you'll have to compare this with situations when you have not run a concept test. Did the concept go through iterations? What did the final design look like? Does concept testing yield a more solid, robust design that comes out better when you do some sort of benchmarking? In that case, how do you measure things like "solid" and "robust"? One way of solving this problem is to tie the designs with some sort of a usability metric that is in turn measured by tangible things like the number of support tickets raised pertaining to usability. An example of one such ticket would be "building a group on my online chat tool is extremely complex." The word "complex" can be used as a proxy to determine the usability of the product. If, by means of running user tests and performing iterative designs, you are actually reducing occurrences of the word "complex" in support tickets, then that's a measure of a return on the investment of research.

You can also evolve your own usability metric. You could assess this via a simple question before the test begins. Ask the participants to rate the usability of the product with a number on a simple scale. Then conduct the test. Use the findings from the test to inform design changes. Implement the design changes, and run the question again by the same set of participants. If they rate the usability of the product higher on the same scale, then behold! Your test has yielded measurable returns.

The issue is that far too often, proxy measures like usability metrics seldom convince people who are looking for an actual dollar amount to justify the need for research in their company. Try convincing them that this doesn't make sense. Even if you were to conjure up a dollar amount, there is no way you can clearly state that the entire amount was only the result of running user research. If the stakeholders still aren't convinced and want you to show them a dollar amount as a return, you should consider quitting your job and joining another company. You deserve better.

16

It's time to fly

Conclusion

"Wow! I had no idea you could do all these things with research. You have an incredibly interesting job."

—AN ENGINEER TO ME

"You are not just a researcher. You are actually a strategist. Where would I hire someone like you?"

—A TRAVELING COMPANION IN AN AIRPLANE TO A USER RESEARCHER WHO HAD JUST EXPLAINED WHAT HE DID FOR A LIVING

Whew! That was some journey, huh?

As a couple of researchers, we have been through a lot, you and I! It's almost time to say good-bye and part ways. But before you leave, I have one last thing for you. It's taken from the story of Mortimer Doormatt Snipple and the product manager he works with, Rob Doesntgivetwohoots. I gave you one version of their story in the introduction. Now, I'm going to give you another. But this time, things are a little different. Well, to be perfectly honest, this second version is not really a story. It's more like an exercise. Here's what I've done. I'm giving you a situation that might exist in their world. I'd like you to use that situation as a context. In tune with today's hyper-customized world, I'm letting you decide what happens next! I am going to present two situations. Then I'll give you some options. You get to choose which of the options you want to go with.

Mortimer Doormatt Snipple is a user researcher who works for a Fortune 500 company. He has recently started working with the product manager, Rob Doesntgivetwohoots.

It is a fine Wednesday morning. Mort is sitting at his desk, thinking about all the amazing things he is going to do the rest of the day. Rob drops by.

Rob could say one of three things to Mort. Choose one that you think is the most likely thing Rob will say.

1. *"Ma-man, ma brotha from anotha motha. How you doin', neighbor?"* He says this because Mort, whose contribution is considered invaluable, is also a part of the product team and sits right next to Rob.

2. *"How you been, man? I haven't seen you in, like, forever."* He says this because Mort has been out of sight and therefore out of Rob's mind. Mort, the only researcher supporting the entire product team, sits on a different floor, along with some new interns.

3. *"Hey there, Chuck...sorry...don't tell me...Mort, is it? I didn't know you still worked here. Good to see you, man!"* He says this because there are some rumors going around that the company's doing some layoffs. All nonessential personnel are being let go. Rob was *sure* Mort had been one of them.

Did you make your choice? Was it 1, 2, or 3? Now if you were in Mort's place, and someone like Rob was the product manager, how do you think he would greet you? If you chose 2 or 3 (I hope you didn't have to choose 3), what do you think needs to change in your organization, and in your relationship with people like Rob for him to greet you like he does in 1? (Well, not exactly with the same words, but with the same warmth—you know what I mean.) More importantly, what can you do to change the situation existing in yourself, your team, and your organization? I would like you to come up with some clear, tangible things you can do to change things. And you'll do yourself an enormous favor if you implement even one of them!

Here's another situation. This time, Rob is speaking with Dave, the design manager you encountered in chapter 14.

Rob and Dave are discussing a pretty gnarly problem. They are in a heated discussion over what a key feature of the product should look like. Dave's design team has come up with a design idea that Rob doesn't seem to like a whole lot. Rob feels that the design is oversimplified and dumbs down a lot of concepts. Dave feels that you can never make a product too simple, and that the simpler designs would in fact reduce the number of customer-support calls that irate customers make when they can't figure something out. And just to make things more fun, in this case, you are the researcher. One of three things can happen next. Your choice.

1. Dave and Rob resolve the issue by themselves. You would have loved to get involved, but they didn't ask you. So you just sigh, keep quiet, and continue working on the script of your next usability test.

2. Dave and Rob come to you to break the tie. You hear them out. Then you narrow your eyes and have that far-away look as you think deeply. Dave and Rob wait patiently, even reverently, for you to finish your thinking. Then you address Rob. "Well, I was the guy who advised Dave to come up with these designs. It's in tune with what I've been saying all long, guys. I have already done extensive exploratory research in this area. The new customer segment we're planning to target with these designs needs the product to be much simpler. They are not like our existing customers at all. In fact, I've already had this conversation with the heads of marketing and brand. In addition to changing the product direction, we're also going to be changing our messaging and targeting strategies. So please stay tuned for more updates."

3. Dave tells Rob that since you report to him, he's had you do a ton of usability testing on the product. The users seem to prefer what Rob calls "dumbed-down" designs more than the more complex version that Rob wants. He sends the link of your report to Rob, who says he'll read it when he has some time.

Again, what do you think is most likely to happen in your company? When I showed this exercise to a researcher-friend of mine, she said that choice 2 is not likely to happen. "That's just not possible," she said. "I've never seen a researcher have that kind of power." I beg to differ. Such situations do exist. Such researchers do exist. I have seen researchers like that with my own eyes. Trust me when I say that. The question is, if you didn't choose choice 2, why not? What's happening in your organization that precludes someone like you from having that kind of power? And again, what can you do about it? How can you influence things so that something like that could happen in *your* life?

This is where a lot of researchers I know would go "I just can't do that!" Here's what I say to them. And to you. Remember the first two sections of the book you just read? The purpose of both these sections is to show that your success, and the success of research as a function in your company, actually depends on you for the most part. It's all about you, you, you. You have the power. You may just not know it yet.

This book is meant to wake you up to two things—the fact that things may not be going swimmingly in your world, and that you can bring about the change. Mahatma Gandhi said, "Be the change that you wish to see in the world." What he meant was that the change begins with you.

So the next time you go into work, think about what you are going to change. It could be one small thing. It could be something within yourself, or in your team. That's OK. Start small. Then move on to bigger things. But on the way, don't forget to enjoy your small successes. Then, spread your wings and fly. Fly high. You can do it.

It's been real, my friend. Good luck with your research.

References

CHAPTER 1
1. 2008 BART Station Profile Study. Accessed 12/3/17 https://www.bart.gov/about/reports/profile

2. New Train Car Project. Accessed 12/3/17 http://www.bart.gov/about/projects/cars

3. Van Kleef, E., Van Triip, H.C.M., and Luning, P. (2005). Consumer research in the early stages of new product development: a critical review of methods and techniques. *Food Quality and Preference,* 16(3): 181–201.

4. Durling, D. (1999) Intuition in Design. *Bulletin of 4th Asian Design Conference International Symposium on Design Science.*

5. Sandler-Smith, E., and Shefy, E. (2004). The intuitive executive: Understanding and applying 'gut feel' in decision-making. *Academy of Management Perspectives*, 18(476–91).

CHAPTER 3
6. *Net Promoter score: The Basics.* Accessed 12/3/17. https://www.satmetrix.com/nps-score-model/

7. Heiman, G. *Basic Statistics for the Behavioral Sciences.* Wadsworth Publishing.

8. NPS Benchmarks. Accessed 12/3/17 https://npsbenchmarks.com/companies.

CHAPTER 4
9. Insight. In *Cambridge.* Accessed 12/3/17. *dictionary.* http://dictionary.cambridge.org/us/dictionary/english/insight#translations.

10. Insight, in *Merriam-Webster dictionary*. Accessed 12/3/17. https://www.merriam-webster.com/dictionary/insight.

11. Insight, in *The Free dictionary*. Accessed 12/3/17. http://www.thefree-dictionary.com/insight.

12. *About APA*. Accessed 12/3/17. http://www.apa.org/support/about-apa.aspx.

13. Vranica.S. Average tenure of CMO continues to decline. *The Wall Street Journal*. Accessed 12/3/17. https://www.wsj.com/articles/average-tenure-of-cmo-continues-to-decline-1489777765.

14. More than one way to skin a cat in *World Wide Words*. Accessed 12/3/17. http://www.worldwidewords.org/qa/qa-mor1.htm.

CHAPTER 5

15. Basadur, M. *How might we? Three simple words that can drive economic prosperity in turbulent times*. Accessed 12/3/17. http://www.basa-dur.com/insightsresearch/OurThoughtsonCreativityandInnovation/HowMightWe/tabid/164/Default.aspx

16. Lebowitz, S. (2017, July 19). Google and Facebook still use the 3-word question that saved a $225 billion company in the 1970s. *Business Insider*. Accessed 12/3/17. http://www.businessinsider.com/how-might-we-questions-2017-7.

CHAPTER 6

17. Market Research vs. Marketing Research—What's the difference? [web blog post]. Accessed 12/3/17. https://www.qualtrics.com/blog/market-research-v-marketing-research/.

18. Kaufman, L., and Rousseeuw, P.J., (2005). *Finding Groups in Data—An Introduction to Cluster Analysis.* Wiley Interscience.

19. Green, P.E., and Srinivasan, V., (1990). Conjoint Analysis in Marketing: New developments with implications for research and practice. The Journal of Marketing, 54(4), 3–19.

CHAPTER 7

20. Burns, M. (2011, August 25). The 7 Iconic Patents That Define Steve Jobs. TechCrunch. Accessed 12/3/17. https://techcrunch.com/2011/08/25/the-7-iconic-patents-that-define-steve-jobs/

21. iPhone X environmental report (September 12, 2017). Accessed 12/3/17. https://images.apple.com/environment/pdf/products/iPhone/iPhone_X_PER_sept2017.pdf.

22. Damasio, A. (2005). *Descarte's Error: Emotion, Reason, and the Human Brain.* Penguin Books, Reprint Edition.

23. Damasio, A. (2009, August 11). *Why emotions make better decisions.* Accessed 12/3/17. https://www.youtube.com/watch?v=1wup_K2WN0I.

CHAPTER 8

24. Tombaugh, C. W. (1946). The Search for the Ninth Planet, Pluto, *Astronomical Society of the Pacific Leaflets,* (Vol. 5, No. 209) pp.73–80.

25. Brown, M.E., Trujillo, C.A., Rabinowitz, D.L. (2005), Discovery of a Planetary-Sized Object in The Scattered Kuiper Belt. *The Astrophysical Journal,* 635: L97–L100.

26. Tindol, R. (6/14/2007). The Dwarf Planet Known as Eris is More Massive than Pluto, New Data Shows. *Caltech news.* Accessed 12/3/17. http://www.caltech.edu/news/dwarf-planet-known-eris-more-massive-pluto-new-data-shows-1293.

27. Editor: Phillips, T. (7/29/2005). 10th Planet Discovered. *NASA Science Beta.* Accessed 12/3/17. https://science.nasa.gov/science-news/science-at-nasa/2005/29jul_planetx.

28. International Astronomical Union Press Release (2006, August 24). Accessed 9/10/17. https://www.iau.org/news/pressreleases/detail/iau0603/ on September 10, 21017.

29. Rosenman, M.F. (2001). Serendipity and Scientific Discovery. *Creativity and Leadership in the 21st century firm.* Vol. 13. PP. 187–193.

30. Bryan, B. (2016). Here's what happened to stocks when the Cubs and the Indians last won the World Series. Business Insider. Nov 2, 2016. Accessed 9/10/17. http://www.businessinsider.com/chicago-cubs-cleveland-indians-world-series-game-7-stock-market-2016-11.

31. Tabachnick, B.G. and Fidell, L.S., (2006). Using Multivariate Statistics (5th Edition). New York City, NY. Pearson.

CHAPTER 10

32. Vlaskovits, P. (2011). Henry Ford, Innovation and That "Faster Horse" Quote. Accessed 8/29/17. *Harvard Business Review*, August 29.

33. The History of the *Rubik's* Cube. Accessed 12/3/17. https://www.rubiks.com/about/the-history-of-the-rubiks-cube/.

34. Brown, S., (2005) Science, serendipity and the contemporary marketing condition, *European Journal of Marketing* 39/11–12: 1229–1234.

35. Eric Ries. *The Lean Startup: How Today's Entrepreneurs Use Continuous Innovation to Create Radically Successful Businesses.* Crown Business. 2011.

36. Ries, E. Building the Minimum Viable Product. Stanford eCorner. **Accessed 12/3/17**. https://ecorner.stanford.edu/2295.ect.

37. Altman, J.K., (2014). To Market Successfully, Your Customer Can't Be 'Everyone' (Op-Ed). *Business News Daily*: Feb 10, 2014.

38. Tommy John Men's Underwear Study Reveals Relationship Men Have with Their Underwear. Accessed 12/3/17. http://www.businesswire.com/news/home/20160212005146/en/Tommy-John-Men%E2%80%99s-Underwear-Survey-Reveals-Relationship.

39. Christensen, C.M., Anthony, S.D. and Roth, E.A. *Seeing what's Next: Using the Theories of Innovation to Predict Industry Change.* Boston: Harvard Business School Press. 2004. Print.

40. Moogk, D.R., (2012). Minimum Viable Product and the Importance of Experimentation in Technology Startups. *Technology Innovation Management Review.* March 2012: 23–26.

CHAPTER 11
41. Dave Morris: The way of Improvisation. Accessed 12/3/17. https://www.youtube.com/watch?v=MUO-pWJ0riQ.

CHAPTER 12
42. Lindstrom, M (2017). *Small Data: The Tiny Clues That Uncover Huge Trends.* Picador.

CHAPTER 13
43. The 21 Most Creative Job Titles. Accessed 12/3/17. http://www.forbes.com/sites/joshlinkner/2014/12/04/the-21-most-creative-job-titles/

CHAPTER 14

44. Definition of Marketing Research. Accessed 12/3/17. https://www.ama.org/AboutAMA/Pages/Definition-of-Marketing.aspx.

About the author

Dilip Chetan started his higher education with a bachelor's degree in electronics engineering. Shortly after he got his engineering degree, an astrologer predicted that he would never study again. Either to prove the astrologer wrong or because had nothing better to do with his time and whatever little money he had, he went on to acquire three master's degrees—an MBA, a masters in computer science, and a masters in human factors psychology. He was also interested in pursuing another degree in fine arts, but he had to stop studying when his wife threatened to divorce him if he enrolled in one more course.

It was during his student days at the University of South Dakota that he discovered his true calling. The field of human factors opened him up to the fascinating world of user research. He discovered that people are seldom able to articulate why they do what they do; it was left to the researcher to deduce by using a variety of techniques. He realized he was good at getting to the underlying motivations that led to different patterns of observable behaviors. He decided to hone these skills and pursue a career in human factors.

Over the course of his career, Dilip has done everything from managing design and research teams to conducting user research for all facets of product development. He has helped implement best practices, conducted workshops on decision-making with top executives, and created a corporate culture where evidence-based product development is valued. His insights have changed the entire strategy of key products in more than one large enterprise. Ever the quirky scientist, he has conducted experiments to assess the impact of loud, aggressive music on driving; studied what happens to people's skin conductance levels when he shocked them by bursting fireworks near them; drove 4,200 miles in six days across the United States just to see how far he could go in a rental minivan with his family (including two five-month-old babies); and, on one odd occasion, posed as an Amish man on a dating website, all in the name of science!

Dilip Chetan currently lives in the Bay Area of California with his wife and twin children.

Index

Made in the USA
San Bernardino, CA
04 May 2018